PER I NIPOTE
ADRIANA E LIDIA
BUON VIÁGGIO
BACI CARI
NÓNNA

ITALIAN
à la Cartoon

Edited by
Albert H. Small, Ph.D.

with the assistance of
Maurizio Fontana

Printed on recyclable paper

PASSPORT BOOKS
a division of *NTC Publishing Group*
Lincolnwood, Illinois USA

Dedicated to
Melanie
Who understands the romance
in the Romance languages

1997 Printing

Published by Passport Books, a division of NTC Publishing Group
© 1996 by NTC Publishing Group, 4255 West Touhy Avenue,
Lincolnwood (Chicago), Illinois 60646-1975 U.S.A.
Manufactured in the United States of America.

7 8 9 VP 0 9 8 7 6 5 4 3 2

Contents

A—Careful!—Word in Advance

Two thousand years ago the Roman Empire was the center of the Western world. The Empire carried Rome's language—Latin—north, south, east, and west. With the fall of the Empire, the "Romance" languages—including French, Spanish, and Italian—developed as locally spoken dialects of Latin.

In Italy, the center of the Roman Empire, ten centuries passed before the new language was used in writing: this language was the *volgare,* the offspring from Latin spoken by most of the people. Initially, educated people were criticized for using the popular language, and many, including the Church, insisted that Latin was the only acceptable language of learning.

The Renaissance, which occurred during the fourteenth to sixteenth centuries, changed this. Great Italian literary figures, including Dante (1265–1321), Petrarch (1304–1374), and Boccaccio (1313–1375), and later Castiglione (1478–1529), Ariosto (1474–1533), and Machiavelli (1469–1527), wrote in Italian, and in a form comprehensible to most Italians today.

The Italian language is now spoken by about 65 million people, chiefly in Italy, but also in the "Ticino" region of Switzerland (where it is one of the official languages) and in some regions of neighboring countries, including France and what was formerly Yugoslavia. There are also large Italian-speaking communities in the Western Hemisphere, including the United States, Argentina, and Canada.

Italy has been a unified nation for more than a century, but local Italian dialects from north to south differed so much that communication between natives of different areas was often difficult, if not impossible. Standard Italian—particularly in written form—developed from the Tuscan dialect. Italy's cultural and literary life centered in Florence (in Tuscany), which overshadowed other cultural centers such as Umbria, where Italian was used in religious writing, and Sicily, the home of the "Sicilian school" of poetry. Today standard Italian dominates the nation, promoted by its use in leading periodicals and, of course, on radio and television. Since World War II, it is Rome, rather than Florence, that most influences Italian speech and writing. *Lingua toscana e favella romana:* Tuscan language and Roman speech.

Italian is a musical-sounding language. It lacks groupings of hard-to-pronounce consonants (as in, for example, the English words *desks, slips, straits*). Instead, many syllables have a single consonant and vowel, and almost all words end in a vowel. And what you see spelled in Italian is what you pronounce. With just a few easy pronunciation rules, you can say whatever you can read.

English is filled with words of Italian origin. Military terms borrowed from Italian include *infantry, artillery, battery, battalion, brigade, corporal, captain, colonel,* and *general.* Architecture borrowed *villa, cupola,* and *balcony.* For other words of Italian origin, look for words ending in *o,* such as *studio, ghetto, cameo, scenario, fiasco, inferno, motto, manifesto, solo,* and *incognito.* Also look for words ending in *a,* such as *influenza, gala, replica, aria, stanza,* and *vista.*

But not all Italian-derived words mean the same thing in English as in Italian. *Confetti*—in English, paper streamers used in celebrations—means a type of candy in Italian.

In return, Italian has been borrowing from English. Some words, such as *bistecca* for "steak" and *supermercato* for "supermarket," have been Italianized, but others like *marketing,* as well as many other business and computer terms, are used unchanged in Italian. Other English words have come into Italian via French: *vagone* (wagon) for a railroad car, *smoking* for a dinner jacket, and *cocktail* for cocktail party.

Music was one of the gifts that Italy gave to the Western world—just think of grand opera! If you have studied music, you already have some Italian vocabulary since Italian words are used in musical notation. Here are some examples:

adagio	slowly
allegro	cheerful
andante	continuous, moderately slow

tempo	time
cantabile	singable
con brio	with spirit
finale	ending
forte	strong
largo	broad
libretto	booklet
moderato	moderate
molto	much
non troppo	not too much
presto	soon
sempre	always, still
subito	sudden
tutti	everybody
vivace	lively

If you have studied Latin, you will recognize many Italian words. Latin words made their way into Italian in one of two ways: (1) through the *volgare,* which, as you have seen, was the spoken language that evolved into today's Italian language and (2) "transplanted" through literary writing such as in scholarly or Church writings. In some cases, the same Latin word made it into Italian through both paths, resulting in two different Italian words derived from the same original Latin word.

The following table shows instances in which two Italian words were derived from the same Latin word. Both Italian words mean about the same:

Latin Word	Italian Words	Meaning
rapidus	rapido, ratto	rapid, swift
nitidus	nitido, netto	distinct, clear
frigidus	frigido, freddo	frigid, cold
quietus	cheto, quieto	quiet
computare	contare, computare	count, compute
talpa	topo, talpa	mouse, mole
regalis	reale, regale	royal
justitia	giustezza, giustizia	correctness, justice

In the following examples, the Latin has Italian derivatives with different meanings:

Latin	Italian	Meaning	Italian	Meaning
examen	sciame	swarm, flock	esame	examination
sagma	soma	burden	salma	body, corpse
collocare	coricare	put to bed	collocare	find employment
atomus	attimo	moment	atomo	atom
causa	cosa	thing	causa	cause

If you have studied French or Spanish, you will find some similarities in Italian. Nouns have in Italian two genders—masculine and feminine—and adjectives agree with nouns. But unlike French and Spanish, which like English add -s or -es to form plurals, Italian plurals do not add -s. Instead, the last vowel in the word changes. For example, for masculine singular endings of -o, substitute -i to form the plural (*gatto, cat; gatti, cats*). For feminine singular endings of -a, substitute -e to form the plural (*casa, house; case, houses*). Like English, French, and Spanish, Italian uses certain auxiliary (helper) verbs such as *essere* (to be) and *avere* (to have) to form certain tenses.

Even if you have studied other Romance languages, Italian will have some surprises for you—for example, the definite article. The definite article is *the* in English; *le, la,* or *les* in French; *el, la, los,* or *las* in Spanish. In Italian, however, the definite article has enough variations to merit its own table in the grammar section that follows in this book. Why this variation? Because speakers of *volgare* had a tendency to use stress and emphasis in their language, so that objects kept being referred to as "this thing" or "that thing"—with the demonstrative pronoun. Eventually *this* and *that* became *the,* and the Italian language had to invent a new set of demonstrative pronouns, with the definite article keeping its varied forms.

Suffixes are a rich resource in the Italian language. Some of them you probably are already familiar with: for example, -issimo, meaning "greatest" or "most," as in *fortissimo* and *generalissimo.* You also know *-etti* and *-elli,* which are diminutives, meaning "little." When you go to an Italian restaurant, you may order spaghetti ("little strings," from *spago [string]* + *etti*) or *vermicelli* ("little worms," from *verme [worm]* + *elli*).

Suffixes can be attached to nouns, adjectives, and even verbs. Four common uses of suffixes are to describe something as "small," "large," "nice," or "nasty." Here are some examples:

The Italian word *vita* means "life." Add *-accia,* and *vitaccia* means a "rotten life."

The word *lupo* means "wolf." Add *-atto,* and *lupatto* means "wolf cub."

Strada means "street." Add *-icciola,* and *stradicciola* means "lane."

Medico means "doctor." Add *-onzolo,* and *mediconzolo* means "second-rate doctor."

Scrittore means "writer." Add *-ucolo,* and *scrittorucolo* means "hack writer."

Bambino means "child." Add *-occio,* and *bamboccio* means "a rag doll" or "a simple person."

The cartoons in this book were chosen because the humor can be translated into English from Italian. For example, the Italian word for *spice*—something to add zest to your life or a kitchen ingredient—can be confused in either English or Italian, with disastrous results. See the cartoon about the little rabbit.

But note well: the literal translation of the cartoon and the "Everyday English" caption given for a cartoon can be quite different. In effect, what we have sometimes done is to recaption the cartoon as an American editor might in adapting an Italian cartoon for an American newspaper or magazine. This not only improves the joke, but often sharply illustrates the difference between Italian and English conversational idioms. And that's the purpose of the book: to help take you away from the routine rules of syntax and vocabulary and bring you out to the world of people speaking Italian in ordinary circumstances. In addition, to make the pages easier to read, we have usually repeated the artist's lettering in the caption under the cartoon.

Why use humor as a learning aid? Obviously because humor is an enjoyable way of getting anything done. But more than that: the key to learning is *memory*—and for almost everybody, there is nothing more memorable than a good joke.

So please don't blame us if you remember the Italian word for *codfish* by associating it with the chef desperately using a fishing pole to fill orders for fish in his restaurant. Or if you associate the Italian word for *dinner* with the condemned man who has to do without it because his execution has been postponed. Or if the Italian word for *fleas* reminds you of the dog lonely without them. Not to mention the Italian for *life imprisonment* reminding you of the cautious fiancée contemplating marriage.

Good reading—good laughing!

A Technical Comment—or Two

Learning a language can be fun, especially when it helps you understand the punch line of a joke or the conversation at a get-together. But let's face it—learning a language can also get complicated. In this book, we're going to try to keep as much of the fun as we can, and burden you with a minimum of complications.

Basically, the vocabulary provided in this book is an aid to understanding the cartoons. We won't give you *all* the possible translations of an Italian word—just the ones that relate to the material at hand. Also, sometimes not all words you may need are given. For example, basic words are explained on the following pages. You can use the Italian-English Glossary at the end of the book to find the meanings of words not defined on the page.

And we won't bother translating the words you can figure out for yourself from English words—even in cases where the spelling differs somewhat from the spelling in English. But be alert for the different ways in which such words can be used in Italian.

Incidentally, we have used some fairly obvious abbreviations:

n.	for noun	adj.	for adjective
v.	for verb	adv.	for adverb
m.	for masculine	prep.	for preposition
f.	for feminine	conj.	for conjunction
sing.	for singular	inf.	for infinitive
pl.	for plural		

To help you recognize a verb in other contexts, we add the infinitive form (when the infinitive isn't used in the cartoon caption) along with the verb form that is used.

For plural nouns whose singular doesn't end in -o (for masculine nouns) or -a (for feminine nouns), the singular form is given.

To avoid cluttering up the vocabulary list under each cartoon, we are including the charts that follow to help you handle the most common words.

- The *Definite Article* has a number of forms so we have shown them in a special table.

- *Pronouns* are an important part of everyday speech, so you need to be familiar with all the common ones.

- *The Three Important Verbs* are important for themselves and as helper (auxiliary) verbs. They are the two verbs for *to be* (*essere* and *stare*) and the verb *to have* (*avere*). You will want to recognize all their forms on sight.

- Finally, *Little Words* are the ones that link together ordinary speech—words such as *but, in, above, because,* and so on.

Rather than listing these words every time they appear in a cartoon caption, we've brought them all together in this list to encourage you to make sure they are a basic part of your Italian vocabulary.

The Definite Article—*the*

	Masculine		Feminine	
	*Before Consonant**	*Before Vowel*	*Before Consonant*	*Before Vowel*
Sing.	il	l'	la	l'
Pl.	i	gli	le	le

	Combinations			
with **a**	al	all'	alla	all'
("to the")	ai	agli	alle	alle
with **di**	del	dell	della	dell'
("of the")	del	degli	delle	delle
with **con**	col	coll'	colla	coll'
("with the")	coi	cogli	colle	colle
with **da**	dal	dall'	dalla	dall'
("from the")	dai	dagli	dalle	dalle
with **in**	nel	nell'	nella	nell'
("in the")	nei	negli	nelle	nelle
with **su**	sul	sull'	sulla	sull'
("on the")	sui	sugli	sulle	sulle

---

*Note: Before certain "s" or "z" sounds, these forms are used: lo, gli; allo, agli; dello, degli; collo, cogli; dallo, dagli; nello, negli; sullo, sugli.

Pronouns

This is not an exhaustive list of pronouns in Italian. Rather, it is an illustration of how common pronouns you will encounter in the cartoon captions can be used in conversation.

Subject Pronouns

io parlo	**I** talk
tu parli	**you** talk
egli or **lui** parla	**he** talks
lei or **essa** parla	**she** talks
Lei *(formal)* parla	**you** talk
noi parliamo	**we** talk
voi parlate	**you** *(plural)* talk
loro or **essi** parlano	**they** *(masculine)* talk
loro or **esse** parlano	**they** *(feminine)* talk
Loro *(formal)* parlano	**you** talk

Direct Object Pronouns

lei **mi** chiama	she calls **me**
lei **ti** chiama	she calls **you**
io **lo** chiamo	I call **him**
io **la** chiamo	I call **her**
io **La** *(formal)* chiamo	I call **you**
lei **ci** chiama	she calls **us**
loro **vi** chiamano	they call **you**
io **li** chiamo	I call **them** *(masculine)*
io **le** chiamo	I call **them** *(feminine)*
io **Li** *(masculine—formal)* chiamo	I call **you**
io **Le** *(feminine—formal)* chiamo	I call **you**

Indirect Object Pronouns

tu **mi** dai la matita	you give **me** the pencil
io **ti** do la matita	I give **you** the pencil
egli **gli** dà la matita	he gives **him** the pencil
lei **le** dà la matita	she gives **her** the pencil
egli **Le** *(formal)* dà la matita	he gives **you** the pencil
tu **ci** dai le matite	you give **us** the pencils
noi **vi** diamo le matite	we give **you** the pencils
noi diamo **loro** le matite	we give **them** *(masculine or feminine)* the pencils
loro danno **Loro** *(formal)* le matite	they give **you** the pencils

Demonstrative and Possessive Pronouns

quello è **il mio**	**that one** is **mine**
questo è **il tuo**	**this one** is **yours**
quello è **il suo**	**that one** is **his**
questi sono **i nostri**	**these** are **ours**
quelli sono **i vostri**	**those** are **yours**
questi sono **i loro**	**these** are **theirs**

Note: The above forms can also be used as adjectives.

Relative Pronouns

che	**what, which**
chi	**who**
con **quale** *(sing.)*	with **whom**
con **quali** *(pl.)*	with **whom**

Three Important Verbs

essere (to be)

Present

io sono
tu sei
egli è
noi siamo
voi siete
loro sono

Past (Imperfect)

io ero
tu eri
egli era
noi eravamo
voi eravate
loro erano

Past (Preterit)

io fui
tu fosti
egli fu
noi fummo
voi fosti
loro furono

Future

io sarò
tu sarai
egli sarà
noi saremo
voi sarete
loro saranno

avere (to have)

Present

io ho
tu hai
egli ha
noi abbiamo
voi avete
loro hanno

Past (Imperfect)

io avevo
tu avevi
egli aveva
noi avevamo
voi avevate
loro avevano

Past (Preterit)

io ebbi
tu avesti
egli ebbe
noi avemmo
voi aveste
loro ebbero

Future

io avrò
tu avrai
egli avrà
noi avremo
voi avrete
loro avranno

stare (to be; also to stay, to stand, to live, to be located)

Present

io sto
tu stai
egli sta
noi stiamo
voi state
loro stanno

Past (Imperfect)

io stavo
tu stavi
egli stava
noi stavamo
voi stavate
loro stavano

Past (Preterit)

io stetti
tu stesti
egli stette
noi stemmo
voi steste
loro stettero

Future

io starò
tu starai
egli starà
noi staremo
voi starete
loro staranno

Little Words

a, ad *(prep.)*	to
anche	also, too
c'è	there is/it is
c'era	there was
che *(conj.)*	that
cosa *(n., f.)*	thing
così *(adv.)*	thus
da *(prep.)*	from
di *(prep.)*	of
dopo	after
e, ed	and
già *(adv.)*	already
il	the (see Definite Article table)
in	in, at, into
la	the (see Definite Article table)
ma	but
mai *(adv.)*	ever, never
molto *(adj./adv.)*	much, many
ne	of it, about it
nessuno *(adj./pronoun)*	no one, not any
niente *(pronoun)*	nothing
non	no, not
oppure	or else, otherwise
per	for, in order to
però	but, however
prego	please
prima	first
qualche *(adj.)*	some
qualcosa *(pronoun)*	something
qualcuno *(pronoun)*	someone
quando	when
quello *(adj./pronoun)*	that
questo *(adj./pronoun)*	this
qui, qua	here, there
se *(conj.)*	if
sempre *(adv.)*	always

senza *(prep.)*	without
sí	yes
solo *(adv.)*	only
sotto *(prep.)*	under
su *(prep.)*	on
tutto *(adj./pronoun)*	all, every, each
un	one

Introducing...the Artists!

Born in 1968 in Bari, a town along Italy's southern Adriatic coast in the Apulia region, **MATTEO DECOSMO** completed his studies at the Accademia di Belle Arti of Florence and Bari. His main interest was in theatrical scenery and set design.

Having been a cartoonist on an occasional and spare-time basis, DeCosmo first thought seriously of the field when he learned of our search for Italian cartoons for this volume. Having found how well his work was accepted, he went on to enter a contest for cartoonists in the southern Italian and nearby Mediterranean regions. He was selected as one of the top ten contestants in the Third Salon for Cartoonists and Motion Picture Animators in Bari, and his work appears in the catalog for the event.

Neither of his parents had been an artist, but, as DeCosmo says, "After I was born, they became artists of a sort like all parents in the world."

Reflecting perhaps the Renaissance tradition in Italy, DeCosmo writes, paints, and composes music. His paintings take inspiration from the colors and rhythms of Mediterranean life around him.

It's a good life as DeCosmo describes it: with enough leisure to play soccer under the southern Italian sky, to swim in the blue Adriatic, and to enjoy the abundance of the southern Italian cuisine.

ENZO SCARTON was born in Venice. In 1970, Scarton began his professional career with an animation studio. But from there, he shifted to the world of advertising and publicity. Achieving the position of art director with an advertising agency in Venice, he moved on to become creative director for a major firm in Trieste that markets brandy and liqueurs.

His work includes the development of package designs, as well as numerous commercial campaigns for the various products. The campaigns range from television commercials to ads for newspapers and magazines, as well as posters

and point-of-sale materials for stores. He supervises the work
of artists, photographers, and printers.

But his first love continues to be comic strips. As a history
fan, he combines his hobbies by writing and drawing strips on
various subjects, including the Crusades, the American West,
pirate stories, and futuristic star wars. All this doesn't keep
him from publishing books, working for magazines, or doing
exhibitions.

His versatility is shown in the cartoons in this book, which
were drawn especially for us.

Now that his work is so well known in Italy, maybe some
reader will find him a publisher in the United States.

SAURO CIANTINI lives and works in Tuscany, just a few blocks
from the Duomo, Florence's world-famous cathedral.

He is an illustrator, graphic artist, and producer of the strip
C'era una volta un anatroccolo piccolo brutto e nero . . .
("Once upon a time there was an ugly little black duckling"),
which appears in the Italian weekly publication *Comix*. And in
1994, he was winner of the "Comix Prize" as the best new
author.

He says that he has "fallen in love" with the work of Carl
Banks, whose name is associated with America's most famous
water bird, Donald Duck, as well as that of George Herriman,
the New Orleans native and pioneer comic artist who, almost
a century ago, created the cartoon character Krazy Kat.
His other heroes include Paul Klee, the German expressionist
artist, who also did pen-and-ink drawings, and Vasily
Kandinsky, the Russian artist, whose abstract paintings are
known particularly for their striking use of color.

His favorite techniques include the use of a Bic pen (black
with a rounded point), acrylics, and inks diluted with water
(or Gallo Nero wine!).

Americans will recognize his favorite fruit—watermelon—
and he is an enthusiastic bicycle tourist.

Ambitions? To create a record album cover for the American
guitarist and jazz musician Pat Metheny, to draw a cover for

the *New Yorker,* and to learn how to whistle without using fingers.

DANILO AQUISTI ("DANILO") has been drawing cartoons since the 1950s. His drawings have appeared in all of Italy's most important weeklies, including *Oggi, Grazia, Annabella, Gioia, Europeo, Epoca, Famiglia Cristiana, Topolino,* and *Intrepido.* Outside Italy, his cartoons have been seen in Prague and Madrid.

He studied his craft in Rome: at the Liceo Artistico, the Scuola di Via Margutta, and the Accademia del Nudo San Luca.

His paintings have caused some to ask whether he is a humorist who paints or a painter with a sense of humor!

That sense of humor has marked his career, not always without effect. As an officer in the Italian army, he decided to give his people some activity by dividing the platoon into two teams for a snowball fight (this led to his house arrest!).

Danilo feels that the ideal cartoon is one without words, but fortunately this book has many examples of his work *with* words.

His leisure activities include travel, the study of parapsychology, music, and gambling—whether playing cards or at the casino (but, he insists, only for fun).

He feels that his cartoons, by turning reality upside-down, can occasionally lighten life's daily burdens. And his motto is "Never put off to tomorrow what you can put off to the day after tomorrow."

GIULIANO ROSSETTI ("GIULIANO") published his first cartoon while still a university student. He studied classics and hoped to secure a degree in architecture. However, before he could complete his studies, work became a necessity.

So he spent fifteen years as a manager at a woolen mill. But then he began collaborating with the publishers of several periodicals, and he finally left his job at the woolen mill to earn a living as a cartoonist.

Currently his work appears in *La Repubblica, Guerin*

Sportivo, Diana, Notizie Verdi, Humor Graphic, and *Comix.*
He also has nine books to his credit including *Giuliano
L'Apostata* (Giuliano the Apostate), *Bla Bla Bla,* and *I Ragazzi
del Presidente* (Children of the President).

He has a wife named Lisetta, a son named Matteo, and a cat
named Socrates.

His ambition is to continue at his profession until he gets
terribly sick and dies—at age 134.

ANTONIO DE LUCA ("LUX") has been a professional cartoonist
for over twenty years. His work has included nature studies,
comics, puzzles, and other types of illustrations. Cartoons
by "Lux" have appeared in a variety of publications, including
Cartoonlandia, Tiramolla, Il Sabato, and many puzzle
magazines, including *Facile Enigmistica, Grande Enigmistica*
and *Mondo Enigmistica.* One unusual assignment has been
illustrating the Bulletin of the Italian Mensa Society, part of an
international group of persons with intelligence-test scores
higher than 98 percent of the population.

Although largely self-taught, De Luca attended the Pittura
All'Accademia Belle Arti and the Laboratorio Fumetto. He has
won prizes and honorable mentions at Montepulciano,
Bordighera, Foligno, Tolentino, and Prato. He enjoys travel—
real or imaginary—and says *La vita è stupenda!* (Life is
marvelous!).

ANTONIO TUBINO has been creating humorous drawings for
publication since the age of 20. He began by getting his
cartoons printed in sports magazines and boys' weeklies. The
publications now carrying them are *Riviste dell'Enigmistica,
La Settimana Enigmistica, Radiocorriere-TV, La Tribuna
Illustrata,* and many others.

He attended the Liceo Artistico. His works have been
entered in all of the most important national humor
competitions, securing prizes at Bordighera, Siena, Asti,
Lanciano, Vercelli, and elsewhere.

His favorite leisure-time activity is organizing informal

soccer games with friends and colleagues. He feels his cartoons reflect an incurable optimism and a positive outlook on life. He agrees with the saying, "If there's a solution to the problem, why worry? And if there's no solution, why worry?"

GHINO CORRADESCHI ("GHINO") estimates that perhaps 10,000 of his cartoons have appeared in print over the past quarter-century. His talent is self-taught. His drawings have appeared in such publications as *Corrado Tedeschi Editore, Domenica Quiz, Medical Tribune, Gazzetta dello Sport,* and *Mercato Nautico.* His works have won prizes at many national and international shows including the "Dattero d'Oro" and "Consiglio d'Europa" awards at Bordighera; first prize for sport humor at the International Show at Foligno; and first prize "Madia d'Oro" at Aquila. He has also won prizes several times at the International Show at Tokyo.

What's his hobby? Collecting cartoons!

MARIO DE CARLINI ("DECA") does not come from a family of artists, and he never attended an art school. He began getting his cartoons published while still a youngster. His work has appeared in *Enigmistiche, Corrado Tedeschi Editore, Domenica Quiz, Rizzoli, Club Enigmistico, Cino del Duca, Intrepido, Editrice Universo, E Altri,* and other publications. Hobbies? Sports—and going to the racetracks. Attitude on life? He likes things the way they are!

Matteo DeCosmo

—Qui c'è scritto: quattro merluzzi, un pesce spada, un chilo di
ostriche, due salmoni e . . .

Key Words

scritto (*v.*, scrivere *inf.*)	written
quattro	four
merluzzi (*n., m., pl.*)	codfish
pesce (*n., m.*) spada	swordfish
chilo (*n., m.*)	kilo, kilogram
ostriche (*n., f., pl.*) (*sing.* ostrica)	oysters
due	two
salmoni (*n., m., pl.*)	salmon

Everyday English

"Here are the orders I've written down: Four codfish, one
swordfish, two pounds of oysters, two orders of salmon,
and . . ."

1

—Alt! Riporta via la cena! La sua esecuzione è stata rinviata.

Key Words

alt	stop
riporta (*v.*, riportare *inf.*)	take back
cena (*n.*, *f.*)	dinner
esecuzione (*n.*, *f.*)	execution
è stata rinviata (*v.*, stare *inf.*, rinviare *inf.*) (*passive form*)	has been postponed

Everyday English

"Stop! Take back the dinner—the execution has been postponed!"

Matteo DeCosmo

—Mamma . . . Mamma, a chi tocca questa volta dire che non ci sei?
A me, vero?

Key Words

fitto (*n., m.*)	rent
tocca a (*v.,* toccare *inf.*)	be one's turn
volta (*n., f.*)	turn, time
dire (*v., inf.*)	say
ci sei (*v.,* essere *inf.*)	you are here
vero?	right?

Everyday English

[*The Rent Collector*]
"Mama, Mama, whose turn is it to say you're not home? Mine,
right?"

3

Giuliano

—Con mia moglie non ci parlavamo da 40 anni, poi una sera si è guastato il televisore e ho scoperto che parla solo tedesco.

Key Words

moglie (*n.*, *f.*)	wife
parlavamo (*v.*, parlare *inf.*)	(we) spoke, (we) talked
anni (*n.*, *m.*, *pl.*)	years
si è guastato (*v.*, guastarsi *inf.*) (*reflexive*)	is broken
televisore (*n.*, *m.*)	television set
ho scoperto (*v.*, scoprire *inf.*)	(I) discovered
tedesco (*n.*, *m.*)	German

Everyday English

"For forty years, my wife and I never talked to one another, and then one night the TV broke down and I discovered that she spoke only German."

4

Sauro Ciantini

«Certo che credo all'amore cieco . . .» gli scrisse la fidanzata lontana. «Ogni volta che ti guardo.»

Key Words

certo (*adv.*)	undoubtedly
credo (*v.*, credere *inf.*)	(I) believe
amore (*n.*, *m.*)	love
cieco (*adj.*)	blind
scrisse (*v.*, scrivere *inf.*)	wrote
fidanzata (*n.*, *f.*)	fiancée
lontana (*adj.*)	distant
ogni (*adj.*)	each, every
volta (*n.*, *f.*)	time
guardo (*v.*, guardare *inf.*)	(I) look at

Everyday English

"Sure I believe love is blind," wrote my fiancée from far away, "every time I look at you."

—Oddio . . . L'ho fatto morire dal ridere!

Key Words

Oddio	O + Dio (God): exclamation
ho fatto (*v.*, fare *inf.*)	(I) made
morire (*v.*, *inf.*)	die
ridere (*v.*, *inf.*)	laugh

Everyday English

"Gosh—I made him die laughing!"

Enzo Scarton

Alessio da Lecce

—Non saranno dei gran combattenti, ma devono avere un gran coreografo.

Key Words

gran (*adj.*)	great
combattenti (*n., m., pl.*)	fighters
(*sing.* combattente)	
devono (*v.,* dovere *inf.*)	(they) must
coreografo (*n., m.*)	choreographer

Everyday English

Alessio of Lecce

"They may not be great fighters but they have a fine choreographer."

Danilo

—Cameriere, ho trovato un bottone nelle minestra . . .
—Meno male! Sono tre giorni che lo cerco . . .

Key Words

cameriere (*n., m.*)	waiter
ho trovato (*v.,* trovare *inf.*)	(I) found
bottone (*n., m.*)	button
minestra (*n., f.*)	vegetable soup
meno male	thank goodness
tre	three
giorni (*n., m., pl.*)	days
cerco (*v.,* cercare *inf.*)	(I) look for

Everyday English

"Waiter, I found a button in my soup."
"Wonderful! I've been looking for it for three days . . ."

Matteo DeCosmo

—Chi ha prenotato una visita di controllo ai canini?

Key Words

ha prenotato (*v.*, prenotare *inf.*)	reserved
visita (*n., f.*)	visit, appointment
controllo (*n., m.*)	control, check
canini (*n., m., pl.*)	canine teeth

Everyday English

"Who called for an appointment to check his canine teeth?"

9

Tubino

—Credo non abbia gradito il voto che gli avete assegnato . . .

Key Words

credo (*v.*, credere *inf.*)   (I) believe
non abbia gradito   (he) didn't like
  (*v.*, gradire *inf.*)
voto (*n.*, *m.*)   mark
avete assegnato (*v.*,   (you) had assigned
  assegnare *inf.*)
mostra (*n.*, *f.*) canina   dog show

Everyday English

[*Outside the Dog Show*]
"I don't think he was pleased with the rating you gave him."

Deca

—Mi sembra ipnotizzato!

Key Words

sembra (*v.*, sembrare *inf.*)   seem

ipnotizzato (*v.*, ipnotizzare   hypnotized
   inf.)

Everyday English

"Looks to me as if he's hypnotized."

Matteo DeCosmo

—Non se ne parla nemmeno, caro dottore . . . Dopo la magnifica serata e dopo aver pagato la cena . . . Lasci che paghi io . . . La prego non si disturbi!

Key Words

parla (*v.*, parlare *inf.*)	speak
nemmeno (*adv.*)	not even
caro (*adj.*)	dear
serata (*n.*, *f.*)	evening
aver pagato (*v.*, pagare *inf.*)	having paid
cena (*n.*, *f.*)	dinner
lasci (*v.*, lasciare *inf.*)	let
paghi (*v.*, pagare *inf.*)	pay
si disturbi (*v.*, disturbarsi *inf.*) (*reflexive*)	disturb yourself

Everyday English

"Don't even think of it, my dear friend. After our magnificent evening and after you paid for dinner, let me pay this . . . don't trouble yourself."

Sauro Ciantini

«È vero . . .» gli scrisse la fidanzata lontana. «Penso anch'io che il vero amore duri tutta la vita . . . come l'ergastolo.»

Key Words

vero (*adj.*)	true
scrisse (*v.*, scrivere *inf.*)	wrote
fidanzata (*n., f.*)	fiancée
lontana (*adj.*)	distant
penso (*v.*, pensare *inf.*)	(I) think
anch'io	I also, me too
amore (*n., m.*)	love
duri (*v.*, durare *inf.*)	lasts
vita (*n., f.*)	lifetime
ergastolo (*n., m.*)	life imprisonment

Everyday English

"It's true," wrote my fiancée from far away, "I think that true love lasts a lifetime . . . like life imprisonment."

Enzo Scarton

Innocenzo III

—Fa colpo, no? Il mio commercialista dice però che fa colpo anche su quelli del fisco.

Key Words

fa (*v.*, fare *inf.*) colpo (*n.*, *m.*)	makes an impression
commercialista (*n.*, *m.*)	treasury advisor
dice (*v.*, dire *inf.*)	says
fisco	tax bureau (equivalent of I.R.S.)

Everyday English

Innocent the Third

"Really impressive, right? But my treasury advisor says it also impresses those in the tax bureau."

Matteo DeCosmo

—Ti dico che è una semplice coincidenza se devo partire per la crociata proprio oggi che arriva tua madre . . .

Key Words

dico (*v.*, dire *inf.*)	(I) tell, say
semplice (*adj.*)	simple
coincidenza (*n.*, *f.*)	coincidence
devo (*v.*, dovere *inf.*)	(I) must
partire (*v.*, *inf.*)	leave, depart
crociata (*n.*, *f.*)	crusade
proprio (*adv.*)	just, exactly
oggi (*adv.*)	today
arriva (*v.*, arrivare *inf.*)	arrives
madre (*n.*, *f.*)	mother

Everyday English

"I'm telling you that it's only a coincidence that I have to leave for the Crusade just today when your mother is arriving."

Tante cose ci fanno apprezzare la buona tavola . . . soprattutto la fame!

Key Words

tante (*adj.*)	so many
fanno (*v.*, fare *inf.*)	make
apprezzare (*v.*, *inf.*)	appreciate
buona (*adj.*)	good
tavola (*n.*, *f.*)	table
soprattutto (*adv.*)	especially, above all
fame (*n.*, *f.*)	hunger

Everyday English

"So many things make you appreciate good cuisine . . . especially hunger!"

Danilo

—Siccome costava troppo, sono partito da solo per il viaggio di nozze . . .

Key Words

siccome (*adv.*)	since
costava (*v.*, costare *inf.*)	(it) cost
troppo (*adv.*)	too much
sono partito (*v.*, partire *inf.*)	(I) left
da solo	by myself
viaggio (*n.*, *m.*) di nozze	honeymoon

Everyday English

"Because it would have cost too much (for the two of us), I left for our honeymoon by myself . . ."

Matteo DeCosmo

—Scusate, da che parte si va per tornare al luna park?

Key Words

scusate (*v.*, scusare *inf.*)	excuse us
da che parte	which way
va (*v.*, andare *inf.*)	go
tornare (*v.*, *inf.*)	return
luna park (*n.*, *m.*)	amusement park

Everyday English

"Excuse us, which way back to the amusement park?"

Sauro Ciantini

C'era una volta un gatto di nome Attila!

«Per la vita randagia che facciamo . . .» disse. «Noi gatti abbiamo un sacco di cose in più . . .»
—Pulci soprattutto.
—Mieow!

Key Words

c'era una volta	once upon a time
randagia (*adj.*)	wandering
facciamo (*v.*, fare *inf.*)	(we) do; live (in this context)
sacco (*n., m.*) di	lot of
pulci (*n., f., pl.*) (*sing.* pulce)	fleas

Everyday English

Once upon a time there was a cat named Attila!

"Through the wandering life," he said, "we get many things."
"Especially fleas."
"Meow."

Tubino

—Non avete letto il cartello?

Key Words

avete letto (*v.*, leggere *inf.*)	did you read?
cartello (*n.*, *m.*)	sign
guasto (*adj.*)	broken, out of order

Everyday English

"Didn't you read the sign?"

Matteo DeCosmo

—I casi sono due: o è miope, oppure ha già mangiato qui! . . .

Key Words

casi (*n., m., pl.*)   possibilities
miope (*adj.*)   nearsighted
ha mangiato (*v.,* mangiare   has eaten
    inf.)

Everyday English

"There are two possibilities: either he's nearsighted or he's eaten here before!"

Sauro Ciantini

C'era una volta un leprotto che fuggí dalla campagna . . .

«Ho voglia di novità» disse. «Di nuovi odori!»
E li trovò. Timo, salvia e rosmarino.

Key Words

leprotto (*n., m.*)	rabbit, bunny
fuggí (*v.,* fuggire *inf.*)	fled
voglia (*n., f.*)	wish, desire
novità (*n., f.*)	new thing
odori (*n., f., pl.*) (*sing.* odore)	odors, spice
timo (*n., m.*)	thyme
salvia (*n., f.*)	sage

Everyday English

Once upon a time there was a little rabbit who fled from the countryside . . .

"I need something new," he said, "to add spice to my life." He found it: Thyme, sage, and rosemary spices in the frying pan.

Enzo Scarton

L'ASSEDIO A OTTONE DI GOTTINGA

L'Assedio a Ottone di Gottinga

—Quel Tir di dinamite non promette niente di buono.

Key Words

assedio (*n., m.*)	siege
Tir (*n., m.*)	truck
promette (*v.*, promettere *inf.*)	promises
niente di buono	nothing good

Everyday English

The Siege of Otto of Gottinga

"That truck loaded with dynamite promises nothing good."

Matteo DeCosmo

—Un attimo, Signor Direttore, è vostra moglie: chiede se vi siete messo di nuovo quei calzini bucati, stamattina!

Key Words

attimo (*n., m.*)	moment
moglie (*n., f.*)	wife
chiede (*v.*, chiedere *inf.*)	ask
vi siete messo (*v.*, mettere *inf.*)	did you wear?
di nuovo	again
bucati (*adj.*)	worm-eaten

Everyday English

"One moment, Mr. Director. It's your wife—she wants to know whether you put on those socks with holes in them again this morning."

Matteo DeCosmo

—Non la finiva mai di parlare e così gli ho insegnato a leggere!

Key Words

animali (*n., m., pl.*) (*sing.* animale)	animals
finiva (*v.,* finire *inf.*)	finished
parlare (*v., inf.*)	talk
ho insegnato (*v.,* insegnare *inf.*)	(I) taught
leggere (*v., inf.*)	read

Everyday English

"He never stopped talking, so I taught him to read."

Sauro Ciantini

C'era una volta un gatto opportunista . . .

«Non è vero!» disse. «Faccio sempre un sacco di feste al mio padrone quando lo vedo . . . con la ciotola in mano.»

Key Words

faccio (*v.*, fare *inf.*)	(I) make
feste (*n.*, *f.*, *pl.*)	parties, expressions of joy
vedo (*v.*, vedere *inf.*)	(I) see
ciotola (*n.*, *f.*)	bowl

Everyday English

Once upon a time there was an opportunistic cat . . .

"It's not true," he said, "that I always make a big fuss for my master when I see him . . . with my bowl in his hand."

Matteo DeCosmo

La Guerra di Troia

—Padre, ti presento Elena. L'ho soffiata a Menelao, ma sono convinto che lui ormai, s'è messo l'anima in pace . . . !

Key Words

presento (*v.*, presentare *inf.*)	(I) present
Elena	Helen
ho soffiata (*v.*, soffiare *inf.*)	(I) stole
Menelao	Menelaus
convinto (*adj.*)	convinced
ormai (*adv.*)	by now
s'è messo (*v.*, mettere *inf.*)	got over (something)
l'anima in pace	

Everyday English

The Trojan War

Paris: "Father, I present Helen of Troy. I stole her from Menelaus, but I think by now he's gotten over it."

Enzo Scarton

LA VEDETTA INDIANA

CHE COSA VEDE LA VEDETTA OCCHIO DI LINCE?

MOLTE FOGLIE, UN TRONCO E UN SACCO DI CILIEGIE.

—Che cosa vede la vedetta Occhio di Lince?
—Molte foglie, un tronco e un sacco di ciliegie.

Key Words

che cosa	what thing
vede (*v.*, vedere *inf.*)	sees
vedetta (*n., f.*)	sentinel, scout
lince (*n., f.*)	lynx
foglie (*n., f., pl.*)	leaves
tronco (*n., m.*)	trunk (of tree)
sacco (*n., m.*) di	lot of
ciliegie (*n., f., pl.*) (*sing.* ciliegia)	cherries

Everyday English

The Indian Scout

"What sees Scout Lynx Eye?"
"Many leaves, a tree trunk, and a lot of cherries."

Deca

—Se vuoi farlo felice, parlagli di suo figlio . . .

Key Words

vuoi (*v.*, volere *inf.*)	(you) want
farlo (*v.*, fare *inf.*)	make (him)
felice (*adj.*)	happy
parlagli (*v.*, parlare *inf.*)	talk (to him)
figlio (*n.*, *m.*)	child

Everyday English

"If you want to make him happy, talk to him about his child."

Matteo DeCosmo

—È strano, anche a me è tornata improvvisamente la voglia di riprendere a fumare!

Key Words

strano	strange
anche (*adv.*)	also, too
è tornata (*v.*, tornare *inf.*)	has returned
improvvisamente (*adv.*)	suddenly
voglia (*n.*, *f.*)	wish, desire
riprendere (*v.*, *inf.*)	take up again
fumare (*v.*, *inf.*)	smoke

Everyday English

"It's strange, but suddenly I too feel like smoking again."

Tubino

—Cara, scendo un attimo a prendere le sigarette e torno subito.

Key Words

cara (*n.*, *f.*)	dear
scendo (*v.*, scendere *inf.*)	(I) go down
attimo (*n.*, *m.*)	moment
prendere (*v.*, *inf.*)	get
sigarette (*n.*, *f.*, *pl.*)	cigarettes
torno (*v.*, tornare *inf.*)	(I) will return
subito (*adv.*)	soon

Everyday English

"Dear, I'm going out for cigarettes. I'll be right back . . ."

Ghino

—E ricordati che mi devi dare del "lei"!

Key Words

ricordati (*v.*, ricordarsi *inf.*) (*reflexive*)	remember
devi (*v.*, dovere *inf.*)	(you) must
dare (*v.*, *inf.*) del lei	address formally

Everyday English

"And remember, for me you must use the formal form of address."

Matteo DeCosmo

—Che cos'è quella cartolina?
—Viene da Venezia. È del nostro idraulico: Ci manda i saluti e ci ringrazia di avergli permesso di pagarsi il viaggio, con tutta la famiglia, grazie all'allagamento del nostro bagno!

Key Words

cartolina (*n., f.*)	postcard
idraulico (*n., m.*)	plumber
saluti (*n., m., pl.*)	greetings
ringrazia (*v.,* ringraziare *inf.*)	thank
grazie all'	thanks to
allagamento (*n., m.*)	overflowing

Everyday English

"What's the postcard?"
"It's from our plumber in Venice. He sends us greetings and thanks us for having made it possible for him to pay for the trip with all his family because of our flooded bathroom."

Deca

—Ma non puoi dimenticare di essere un dentista?

Key Words

non puoi (*v.*, potere *inf.*)	can't you?
dimenticare (*v.*, *inf.*)	forget
dentista (*n.*, *m.*)	dentist

Everyday English

"Can't you ever forget you're a dentist?"

Enzo Scarton

IL GENERALE CUSTER

Il Generale Custer

—Guardi che la battaglia non è ancora incominciata, generale.
—E allora? Mi sto preparando psicologicamente.

Key Words

guardi (*v.*, guardare *inf.*)	look
battaglia (*n.*, *f.*)	battle
ancora (*adv.*)	yet
è incominciata (*v.*, incominciare *inf.*)	has begun
allora (*adv.*)	then, in that case
mi sto preparando (*v.*, preparare *inf.*)	(I'm) preparing myself
psicologicamente (*adv.*)	psychologically

Everyday English

General Custer

"Looks like the battle hasn't yet begun, General."
"And in that case I am preparing myself psychologically."

Matteo DeCosmo

—Signora non si preoccupi, ma gli lasci fare ciò che vogliono!
—Lei può lasciare che facciano ciò che vogliono! Io no!

Key Words

si preoccupi (*v.*, preoccuparsi *inf.*)	worry
lasci (*v.*, lasciare *inf.*) fare	let, allow
ciò che (*pron.*)	what(ever)
vogliono (*v.*, volere *inf.*)	(they) want
può (*v.*, potere *inf.*)	(you) can
facciano (*v.*, fare *inf.*)	(they) do

Everyday English

"Madam, don't worry, let them do what they want!"
"You can let them do what they want! I can't!"

Danilo

— . . . E se non avessi avuto qui gli amici con i quali parlare, giuro che sarei impazzito!

Key Words

non avessi avuto (*v.*, avere *inf.*)	(I) had not had
amici (*n.*, *m.*, *pl.*)	friends
parlare (*v.*, *inf.*)	talk
giuro (*v.*, giurare *inf.*)	(I) swear
sarei (*v.*, essere *inf.*) (*conditional form*)	(I) would be
impazzito (*adj.*)	crazy

Everyday English

"If I hadn't had those friends to talk to, I'd certainly have gone crazy!"

Sauro Ciantini

C'era una volta un anatroccolo piccolo brutto e nero . . .

«Vuoi attraversare il Polo Nord tutto da solo?» gli scrisse la fidanzata lontana. «Questa tua mania dell'avventura mi farà morire! dal ridere.»

Key Words

anatroccolo (*n., m.*)	duckling
attraversare (*v., inf.*)	to cross
Polo Nord (*n., m.*)	North Pole
farà (*v.*, fare *inf.*)	will make
morire (*v., inf.*)	die
ridere (*v., inf.*)	laugh
slitta (*n., f.*)	sled

Everyday English

Once upon a time there was an ugly little black duckling . . .

"You want to get to the North Pole all by yourself?" wrote my fiancée from far away. "Your mania for adventure will make me die . . . laughing."

Matteo DeCosmo

—Ma avevo sentito abbaiare un cane!
—Eh, caro mio . . . Al giorno d'oggi se non si sanno le lingue, non si mangia!

Key Words

avevo sentito (*v.*, sentire *inf.*)	(I) had heard
abbaiare (*v.*, *inf.*)	bark
sanno (*v.*, sapere *inf.*)	know
lingue (*n.*, *f.*, *pl.*)	languages

Everyday English

"Meow!"
"Bowwow!"
Mouse: ". . . I heard a dog barking!"
Cat: "Oh, my dear! These days, if you don't know other languages, you don't eat!"

Tubino

—Non lo sa nessuno, che dalla prossima settimana costeranno 18.000 lire . . .

Key Words

nessuno	nobody
sa (*v.*, sapere *inf.*)	knows
prossima (*adj.*)	next
settimana (*n.*, *f.*)	week
costeranno (*v.*, costare *inf.*)	will cost
abbigliamento (*n.*, *m.*)	clothing
ancora (*adv.*)	again, still
articoli (*n.*, *m.*, *pl.*)	articles

Everyday English

Sign: "One more week. All these items only 20,000 lire!"
"Nobody knows that next week everything will cost only 18,000 lire . . ."

Enzo Scarton

LA PISTOLA PIÙ VELOCE DEL WEST

ENZO SCARTON

COME MIRA, NON PRENDEREBBE NEANCHE UN BISONTE DA MEZZO METRO.
COME FORTUNA, PRENDEREBBE SUBITO IL PREMIO OSCAR.

PÙM!

La Pistola Più Veloce del West

Come mira, non prenderebbe neanche un bisonte da mezzo metro.
Come fortuna, prenderebbe subito il premio Oscar.

Key Words

pistola (*n., f.*)	gun
veloce (*adj.*)	fast
mira (*n., f.*)	aim
prenderebbe (*v.*, prendere *inf.*)	could get
bisonte (*n., m.*)	buffalo
mezzo (*adj.*)	half
subito (*adv.*)	soon
premio Oscar (*n., m.*)	Oscar (movie award)

Everyday English

The Fastest Gun in the West

"As far as aim is concerned, he couldn't even get a buffalo at half a yard. As far as luck is concerned, he won his Oscar right away."

—Signor Rossi, avete chiamato voi ieri, per quella piccola perdita al rubinetto?

Key Words

avete chiamato (*v.*, chiamare *inf.*)   (you) had called

ieri (*adv.*)   yesterday

piccola (*adj.*)   small

perdita (*n.*, *f.*)   leak (in this context)

rubinetto (*n.*, *m.*)   faucet

Everyday English

"Mr. Rossi, was it you who called yesterday about the small leak in the faucet?"

Sauro Ciantini

C'era una volta un anatroccolo piccolo brutto e nero . . .

«Vuoi venire a passare le vacanze a casa mia?» gli scrisse la fidanzata lontana. «È stupendo! . . . così potrai innaffiarmi le piante mentre sono al mare.»

Key Words

potrai (*v.*, potere *inf.*)	(you) will be able to
innaffiarmi (*v.*, innaffiare *inf.*)	water (for me)
piante (*n.*, *f.*, *pl.*)	plants
mare (*n.*, *m.*)	sea, seashore

Everyday English

Once upon a time there was an ugly little black duckling . . .

"Would you like to pass your vacation at my house," wrote my fiancée from far away. "It will be stupendous! That way you can water the plants while I'm at the seashore."

Deca

—Carlo, è l'ora di portare Fuffi a passeggio . . .

Key Words

ora (*n., f.*)	hour, time
portare (*v., inf.*)	take out
passeggio (*n., m.*)	walk

Everyday English

"Carlo, it's time to take Fuffi out for a walk . . ."

Matteo DeCosmo

—Non capisco! Hai sempre da ridire su ogni cosa che faccio per tutta la famiglia.

Key Words

non capisco (*v.*, capire *inf.*)	(I) don't understand
ridire (*v.*, *inf.*) su	find fault with
ogni (*adj.*)	every
faccio (*v.*, fare *inf.*)	(I) do
famiglia (*n.*, *f.*)	family

Everyday English

"I don't understand! You always criticize whatever I do for anybody in the family!"

Danilo

—Non sono io che ho sempre ragione: sei tu che hai sempre torto!

Key Words

ho (*v.*, avere *inf.*) ragione   (I) am right
hai (*v.*, avere *inf.*) torto   (you) are wrong

Everyday English

"It's not that I am always right: it's that you are always wrong!"

Enzo Scarton

IL GOVERNATORE FANDANGO Y PASO DOBLE

PRIMA CHE ARRIVASSIMO NOI SPAGNOLI, QUI LA TERRA ERA INCOLTA, NON C'ERA MONETA, NE' BANCHE NE' SUPERMERCATI, NON C'ERANO NE' AUTOSTRADE NE' PARCHEGGI. PER NON PARLARE DEI FAST FOOD. DI CHE TI LAMENTI?

HA APPENA FATTO L'ELENCO.

ENZO SCARTON

Il Governatore Fandango y Paso Doble

—Prima che arrivassimo noi spagnoli qui la terra era incolta, non c'era moneta, né banche, né supermercati, non c'erano né autostrade né parcheggi, per non parlare dei fast food. Di che ti lamenti?
—Ha appena fatto l'elenco.

Key Words

spagnoli (*n., m., pl.*)	Spaniards
incolta (*adj.*)	uncultivated
parcheggi (*n., m., pl.*) (*sing.* parcheggio)	parking lots
ti lamenti (*v.*, lamentarsi *inf.*)	(you) complain

Everyday English

Governor Fandango and Paso Doble

"Before the Spanish arrived, land was not cultivated, there was no money, no banks, no supermarkets, there were no highways or parking lots, not to mention fast-food restaurants. What are you complaining about?"
"That's just the list."

Matteo DeCosmo

—Vorrei qualcosa di romantico da far ascoltare a mio marito quando gli faccio vedere i conti . . .

Key Words

vorrei (*v.*, volere *inf.*)	(I) would like
romantico (*adj.*)	romantic
ascoltare (*v., inf.*)	listen to
marito (*n., m.*)	husband
vedere (*v., inf.*)	see
conti (*n., m., pl.*)	bills

Everyday English

"I'd like something romantic for my husband to listen to while I show him the bills."

Sauro Ciantini

C'era una volta un anatroccolo piccolo brutto e nero . . .

«Come cuoco sai fare veramente di tutto!» gli scrisse la fidanzata lontana. «Soprattutto pasticci!»

Key Words

cuoco (*n., m.*)	cook
sai (*v.,* sapere *inf.*)	(you) know
pasticci (*n., m., pl.*) (*sing.* pasticcio)	casseroles; mess (in this context)

Everyday English

Once upon a time there was an ugly little black duckling . . .

"As a cook you really know how to make everything," wrote my fiancée from far away, "especially a mess!"

Tubino

—No, il mio non è subacqueo, anzi teme tremendamente l'acqua . . .

Key Words

il mio (*possessive pronoun*)	mine
subacqueo (*adj.*)	underwater
anzi (*adv.*)	rather
teme (*v.*, temere *inf.*)	fears
tremendamente (*adv.*)	tremendously
acqua (*n., f.*)	water

Everyday English

"No, not only is mine not waterproof, actually it's terribly afraid of water."

Matteo DeCosmo

—Come ti chiami?
—Adesso mi chiamo Giuseppe! Però fino ad un anno fa, credevo che il mio nome fosse "Zitto".

Key Words

come ti chiami (*v.*, chiamarsi *inf.*)	what is your name?
adesso (*adv.*)	now
fino ad (*prep.*)	until
anno (*n.*, *m.*)	year
fa	ago
credevo (*v.*, credere *inf.*)	believed
nome (*n.*, *m.*)	name
zitto (*interjection*)	shut up, keep quiet

Everyday English

"What's your name?"
"My name is Joseph. But until a year ago I thought my name was 'Shut up!'"

Giuliano

—Si avvertono i signori passeggeri che fra otto minuti inizierà lo sciopero dei piloti. Troverete i paracaduti sotto i sedili.

Key Words

si avvertono (*v.*, avvertire *inf.*)	are warned
inizierà (*v.*, iniziare *inf.*)	will start
sciopero (*n.*, *m.*)	strike
piloti (*m.* or *f.*, *pl.*) (*sing.* pilota)	pilots
troverete (*v.*, trovare *inf.*)	will find
paracaduti (*m.*, *pl.*) (*sing.* paracadute)	parachutes
sedili (*n.*, *m.*, *pl.*) (*sing.* sedile)	seats

Everyday English

"Ladies and gentlemen, in eight minutes the pilots' strike will begin. You'll find the parachutes under the seats."

Tubino

—C'è ancora quel tale che insiste a voler brevettare il suo "sistema di volo con ali posticce" . . .
—Va bene, lo faccia entrare.
—Signore, si accomodi.

Key Words

brevettare (*v., inf.*)	to patent
volo (*n., m.*)	flight
ali (*n., f., pl.*) (*sing.* ala)	wings
posticce (*adj., pl.*)	artificial
faccia (*v.,* fare *inf.*) entrare (*v., inf.*)	let (him) come in

Everyday English

"That person's here again who insists he wants to patent a system to fly with artificial wings."
"All right, send him in."
"Come have a seat, sir."

È il miglior bagnino che abbiamo mai avuto . . .

Key Words

miglior (*adj.*)	best
bagnino (*n., m.*)	lifeguard
abbiamo avuto (*v.*, avere *inf.*)	have had

Everyday English

[*Walking on Water*]

"He's the best lifeguard we've ever had."

Enzo Scarton

I Coloni

—Dunque: Fagioli, pancetta, sale, vanga, piccone, fucile, piatti, pentole, deodorante, Bibbia, dadi per brodo, pigiami, sega, calzini, chiodi e dentifricio. Ci siamo dimenticati niente?
—Dove dobbiamo andare.

Key Words

coloni (*n.*, *m.*, *pl.*) (*sing.* colone)	colonists
ci siamo dimenticati (*v.*, dimenticare *inf.*)	have (we) forgotten
dobbiamo (*v.*, dovere *inf.*)	(we) have to

Everyday English

The Colonists

"Well: beans, bacon, salt, shovel, pick, rifle, dishes, pots, deodorant, Bible, bouillon cubes, pajamas, saw, socks, nails and toothpaste—have I forgotten anything?"
"[Yes.] Where we are going."

Sauro Ciantini

C'era una volta un anatroccolo piccolo brutto e nero . . .

«È vero: viaggiare per il mondo porta via un sacco di tempo . . .» disse. «Mai però come rimettere a posto poi tutte le fotografie!»

Key Words

viaggiare (*v., inf.*)	travel
mondo (*n., m.*)	world
porta (*v.,* portare *inf.*) via	takes away
rimettere (*v.,* rimettere *inf.*) a posto	put in order

Everyday English

Once upon a time there was an ugly little black duckling . . .

"It's true: travelling around the world takes a lot of time," he said, "but especially arranging all the photos afterwards!"

Matteo DeCosmo

—Non perderebbe una partita di calcio per nulla al mondo!

Key Words

non perderebbe (*v.*, perdere *inf.*)	wouldn't miss
partita (*n.*, *f.*)	match
calcio (*n.*, *m.*)	soccer
per nulla	for anything
mondo (*n.*, *m.*)	world

Everyday English

"He wouldn't miss that soccer match for anything in the world!"

Deca

—Sei ancora in collera con me, cara?

Key Words

ancora (*adv.*)   still
collera (*n., f.*)   anger
cara (*n., f.*)   dear

Everyday English

"Still angry with me, dear?"

Tubino

—Cameriere, ho chiesto un caffè forte ma non sino a questo punto!

Key Words

cameriere (*n., m.*)	waiter
chiesto (*v.*, chiedere *inf.*)	(I) asked for
caffè (*n., m.*)	coffee
forte (*adj.*)	strong
sino a (*prep.*)	even to
questo (*adj.*)	this
punto (*n., m.*)	point

Everyday English

"Waiter, I asked for strong coffee, but not *this* strong."

Matteo DeCosmo

—Sento piangere disperatamente. Sono forse i quattro gemelli nati stamattina che urlano?
—No. È il padre.

Key Words

sento (*v.*, sentire *inf.*)	hear
piangere (*v.*, *inf.*)	cry
disperatamente (*adv.*)	desperately
forse (*adv.*)	maybe
quattro gemelli (*n.*, *m.*, *pl.*)	quadruplets
nati (*v.*, nascere *inf.*)	born
stamattina (*adv.*)	this morning
urlano (*v.*, urlare *inf.*)	howl, yell
padre (*n.*, *m.*)	father

Everyday English

"I hear desperate crying. Is the yelling perhaps from the quadruplets born this morning?"
"No, it's their father."

Enzo Scarton

Il Duca Gualtiero

— . . . Allora feci capire a quell'orribile plebeo che un duca è intoccabile e che non poteva permettersi assolutamente di rompermi un braccio!
—E allora?
— . . . Allora mi ha rotto una gamba.

Key Words

feci (*v.*, fare *inf.*)	made
plebeo (*n.*, *m.*)	plebeian
intoccabile (*adj.*)	untouchable
rompermi (*v.*, rompere *inf.*)	break (on me)
ha rotto (*v.*, rompere *inf.*)	has broken

Everyday English

Duke Gualtiero

"And then I explained to that horrible plebeian that a duke is untouchable and I absolutely could not permit him to break my arm."
"And then?"
"And then he broke my leg."

Sauro Ciantini

C'era una volta un anatroccolo piccolo brutto e nero . . .

«Goloso io?!» disse. «No. Goloso proprio no.»
Magari bugiardo.

Key Words

goloso (*adj.*)	gluttonous
proprio (*adj.*)	really
magari (*adv.*)	maybe
bugiardo (*n., m.*)	liar

Everyday English

Once upon a time there was an ugly little black duckling . . .

"Me a glutton?" he said. "No, I'm not a glutton."
Maybe a liar.

Matteo DeCosmo

—Oh, cara, mi dispiace . . . non insistere, ma questa sera non c'è il "Rigoletto" in repertorio!

Key Words

cara (*n., f.*)	dear
mi dispiace (*v.*, dispiacere *inf.*)	(I am) sorry
insistere (*v., inf.*)	insist
questa sera	this evening
repertorio (*n., m.*)	repertoire

Everyday English

"My dear, I'm sorry! . . . Don't insist, because tonight there is no 'Rigoletto' in the repertoire!"

Danilo

—Non posso darLe la mia mano se lei non parla prima con i miei genitori . . .

Key Words

non posso (*v.*, potere *inf.*)	(I) can't
darLe (*v.*, dare *inf.*)	give (you)
mano (*n., f.*)	hand
parla (*v.*, parlare *inf.*)	speak
prima (*adv.*)	first
genitori (*n., m., pl.*) (*sing.* genitore)	parents
legge (*v.*, leggere *inf.*)	read

Everyday English

Palm Reading

"I can't give you my hand unless you first talk with my parents."

Deca

—Non vorrai mica che la faccia solo io la dieta!

Key Words

vorrai (*v.*, volere *inf.*)	(you) want
non . . . mica	not at all
faccia (*v.*, fare *inf.*)	do; be on (in this context)
solo (*adj.*)	alone
dieta (*n.*, *f.*)	diet

Everyday English

"You certainly don't want me to be on this diet all by myself!"

Matteo DeCosmo

—Mia madre è stata invitata ad un cocktail e non è più tornata . . .

Key Words

madre (*n., f.*)	mother
è stata invitata (*v.,* invitare *inf.*) (*passive form*)	was invited
cocktail (*n., m.*)	cocktail party
non più	no more
è tornata (*v.,* tornare *inf.*)	has returned

Everyday English

"My mother was invited to a cocktail party, and she never came back!"

Ghino

—Scommetto che hai di nuovo incontrato qualche indiano.

Key Words

scommetto (*v.,* scommettere *inf.*)	(I) bet
hai incontrato (*v.,* incontrare *inf.*)	(you) met
di nuovo	again
qualche (*adj.*)	some
indiano (*n., m.*)	Indian

Everyday English

"I bet you met an Indian again."

Sauro Ciantini

C'era una volta un anatroccolo piccolo brutto e nero . . .

«Sono sicura che un po' di solitudine . . .» gli scrisse la fidanzata lontana «ti farà crescere sicuramente!»
Di qualche kilo!

Key Words

sicura (*adj.*)	sure
farà (*v.,* fare *inf.*)	will make
crescere (*v., inf.*)	grow
kilo (*n., m.*)	kilogram (about 2.2 pounds)
Nute . . . = Nutella	spread for bread popular in Italy

Everyday English

Once upon a time there was an ugly little black duckling . . .

"I'm sure that a little solitude," wrote my fiancée from far away, "will make you a bigger person."
By some kilos!

Matteo DeCosmo

—Giorgio, ti avevo pregato di non riparare il tetto, proprio oggi che veniva a trovarmi la mamma!

Key Words

avevo pregato (*v.*, pregare *inf.*)	(I) had begged
riparare (*v.*, *inf.*)	repair
tetto (*n.*, *m.*)	roof
proprio oggi	just today
veniva (*v.*, venire *inf.*)	was coming
trovarmi (*v.*, trovare *inf.*)	visit (me)

Everyday English

"George, I begged you not to repair the roof today just when mother was coming to visit!"

Enzo Scarton

IL CROCIATO

Il Crociato

—Per venire alle crociate ho lasciato nel mio feudo tutto quello che c'era.
—E che cosa c'era?
—La peste!

Key Words

crociato (*n.*, *m.*)   Crusader
ho lasciato (*v.*, lasciare *inf.*)   (I) left
peste (*n.*, *f.*)   plague

Everyday English

The Crusader

"To come on the Crusades, I left behind everything in my fiefdom."
"And what was it (you left behind)?"
"The plague!"

Tubino

—Fai attenzione, c'è quel monello che si diverte a tirare palle di neve . . .

Key Words

fai (*v.*, fare *inf.*) attenzione	be careful
monello (*n.*, *m.*)	urchin, brat
si diverte (*v.*, divertirsi *inf.*) (*reflexive*)	amuse (himself)
tirare (*v.*, *inf.*)	throw
palle (*n.*, *f.*, *pl.*) di neve	snowball

Everyday English

"Be careful, that kid is amusing himself throwing snowballs."

Matteo DeCosmo

—Sono spiacente, signore, non facciamo credito, e non accettiamo nemmeno carte di credito per la vendita dei nostri prodotti!

Key Words

bevande (*n., f., pl.*)	beverages
fresche (*adj., pl.*) (*sing. fresco*)	fresh
spiacente (*adj.*)	sorry
facciamo (*v.,* fare *inf.*)	(we) give (in this context)
accettiamo (*v.,* accettare *inf.*)	(we) accept
carte (*n., f., pl.*) di credito	credit cards
vendita (*n., f.*)	sale
prodotti (*n., m., pl.*)	products

Everyday English

"Sorry, sir, we don't give credit, and we don't even accept credit cards for the sale of our products!"

72

Sauro Ciantini

C'era una volta un anatroccolo piccolo brutto e nero . . .

«Con la tua mania di stare sempre davanti alla TV . . . » gli scrisse la fidanzata lontana «ti sei perso un sacco di cose! Il cervello, per esempio.»

Key Words

davanti a (*prep.*)	in front of
sei perso (*v.,* perdere *inf.*)	(you) have lost
cervello (*n., m.*)	brain, mind
per esempio	for instance

Everyday English

Once upon a time there was an ugly little black duckling . . .

"With your mania for staying in front of the TV," wrote my fiancée from far away, "you've lost a lot of things! Your brain, for example."

Danilo

—Abbiamo fatto il possibile, ma per il gilè la stoffa non è proprio bastata!

Key Words

abbiamo fatto (*v.*, fare *inf.*)	(we) have done
possibile (*n.*)	everything possible
gilè (*n.*, *m.*)	vest
stoffa (*n.*, *f.*)	cloth
proprio (*adj.*)	really
è bastata (*v.*, bastare *inf.*)	be enough
sartoria (*n.*, *f.*)	tailor shop

Everyday English

The Tailor Shop

"We have done our best, but there's not enough material for a vest."

Matteo DeCosmo

—Alfredo, con questo, vuoi dirmi che ti hanno aumentato lo stipendio?

Key Words

con questo	with this
dirmi (*v.*, dire *inf.*)	tell (me)
hanno aumentato (*v.*, aumentare *inf.*)	(they) have increased
stipendio (*n.*, *m.*)	salary

Everyday English

"Alfred! What's up? Are you telling me you got a raise?"

Deca

—Fino a quando qualcuno non inventa la televisione qui non si sa come passare il tempo!

Key Words

fino a (*prep.*)	until
inventa (*v.*, inventare *inf.*)	invents
televisione (*n., f.*)	television
sa (*v.*, sapere *inf.*)	knows
come (*adv.*)	how
passare (*v., inf.*)	pass
tempo (*n., m.*)	time

Everyday English

"Until somebody invents television, nobody knows how to pass the time!"

Enzo Scarton

DOC

—Doc, la sai quella della cicciona?
—No. E neanche la voglio sapere.

Key Words

sai (*v.*, sapere *inf.*)	know
cicciona (*n.*, *f.*)	fat lady
neanche (*adv.*)	not even
voglio (*v.*, volere *inf.*)	(I) want, wish

Everyday English

Doc

"Doc, do you know the one about the fat lady?"
"No, and I don't even want to."

77

Matteo DeCosmo

—No, caro, quello no . . . ! Nemmeno quell'altro . . .
neppure . . . Su un po' di fantasia, sforzati ad indovinare!

Key Words

caro (*n., m.*)	dear
nemmeno	not even
quell'altro	that other
neppure (*adv.*)	not even
su	come on
un po' (poco) (*pronoun*)	a little
fantasia (*n., f.*)	imagination
sforzati (*v.,* sforzarsi *inf.*) (*reflexive*)	try hard
indovinare (*v., inf.*)	guess

Everyday English

"No dear! Not that! Not even that! No . . . Use a little
imagination . . . really try to guess!!!"

Sauro Ciantini

C'era una volta un leprotto di campagna . . .

«Se ripenso al bel tempo andato, mi vengono le lacrime . . .» disse.
«Sarà la nostalgia.»
O la cipolla.

Key Words

leprotto (*n., m.*)	young rabbit
ripenso (*v.*, ripensare *inf.*)	think back
bel tempo andato	good old times
lacrime (*n., f., pl.*)	tears
cipolla (*n., f.*)	onion

Everyday English

Once upon a time there was a country rabbit . . .

"To think back to the good old times makes me cry," he said.
"Could it be nostalgia?" Or the onion?

Tubino

—No, signorina, non è regolare che lei risponda anche per il suo fidanzato . . .

Key Words

signorina (*n., f.*)	miss
regolare (*adj.*)	customary
risponde (*v.*, rispondere *inf.*)	respond
anche (*adv.*)	also
fidanzato (*n., m.*)	fiancé

Everyday English

"No, miss, it is not customary for you to also respond for your fiancé."

Matteo DeCosmo

—Venga, venga . . . Faccia con comodo, come se fosse a casa sua . . . Benvenuto sull'isola. Non l'avremmo mai sperato che qualcuno ci facesse visita!

Key Words

venga (*v.*, venire *inf.*)	come
faccia (*v.*, fare *inf.*) con comodo	take your time
se fosse (*v.*, essere *inf.*) a casa sua	as if you were at home
avremmo sperato (*v.*, sperare *inf.*)	would have expected
facesse (*v.*, fare *inf.*) visita	would pay a visit

Everyday English

"Come ashore . . . Take your time, make yourself at home . . . Welcome to our island . . . We never would have expected a visitor!"

Giuliano

—Io e mia moglie ci odiamo ferocemente. Però non divorziamo per non traumatizzare il nostro gatto.

Key Words

moglie (*n., f.*)	wife
ci odiamo (*v.*, odiare *inf.*)	(we) hate each other
ferocemente (*adv.*)	fiercely, a lot
divorziamo (*v.*, divorziare *inf.*)	(we) divorce
traumatizzare (*v., inf.*)	traumatize
gatto (*n., m.*)	cat

Everyday English

"My wife and I *really* hate each other. But we won't get a divorce for fear of traumatizing our cat."

Sauro Ciantini

C'era una volta un cane di nome Blék!

«Da quando mi hanno tolto tutte quelle pulci . . .» disse. «Mi sento davvero più . . . come dire . . .»
—Solo.

Key Words

tolto (*v.*, togliere *inf.*)	taken
pulci (*n.*, *f.*, *pl.*) (*sing.* pulce)	fleas
sento (*v.*, sentire *inf.*)	feel
davvero (*adv.*)	indeed

Everyday English

Once upon a time there was a dog named Blek!

"When I am completely rid of fleas," he said. "I feel a little . . . how to say it . . ." "Alone."

Matteo DeCosmo

—Sai, Enrico . . . I leoni hanno la testa grossa per non passare attraverso le sbarre!

Key Words

sai (*v.*, sapere *inf.*)	(you) know
leoni (*n., m., pl.*)	lions
testa (*n., f.*)	head
grossa (*adj.*)	big
passare (*v., inf.*)	pass
attraverso (*prep.*)	across
sbarre (*n., f., pl.*)	bars

Everyday English

"You know, Enrico, lions have a big head so as not to be able to get through the bars!"

Enzo Scarton

IL RE DI SPAGNA

Il Re di Spagna

—Le nostre colonie sono infestate dai pirati, sire. Bisognerà mandare in quei mari qualcuno senza scrupoli, subdolo, feroce e sanguinario, per debellare il fenomeno.
—Fai le valigie e gonfia il gommone.

Key Words

subdolo (*adj.*)	treacherous, deceitful
sanguinario (*adj.*)	bloodthirsty
debellare (*v., inf.*)	crush
gonfia (*v.,* gonfiare *inf.*)	inflate
gommone (*n., m.*)	rubber boat, raft

Everyday English

The King of Spain

"Our colonies are infested with pirates, sir. We have to send somebody overseas without scruples, treacherous, fierce, and bloodthirsty to crush those people."
"Pack your bags and inflate your boat."

Danilo

DANILO

—Non startene lì muto, Piero! Di' qualcosa in modo che io possa interromperti!

Key Words

startene (*v.*, stare *inf.*)	stay
lì (*adv.*)	there
muto (*adj.*)	silent
di' (*v.*, dire *inf.*)	say
in modo	so that
posso (*v.*, potere *inf.*)	(I) can, could
interromperti (*v.*, interrompere *inf.*)	interrupt (you)

Everyday English

"Don't sit there without speaking, Piero! Say something so that I can interrupt you!"

Matteo DeCosmo

—Cara, ne ho assaggiato qualcuno per assicurarmi che fossero di tuo gradimento!

Key Words

cara (*n., f.*)	dear
ne ho assaggiato (*v.,* assaggiare *inf.*)	(I) tasted (them)
assicurarmi (*v.,* assicurarsi *inf.*) (*reflexive*)	assure myself
fossero (*v.,* essere *inf.*)	would be
gradimento (*n., m.*)	liking

Everyday English

"I tasted some to be sure you would like them!"

Deca

—Se la mia è una malattia immaginaria, non penserà che paghi questa parcella!

Key Words

la mia (*possessive pronoun*)	mine
malattia (*n., f.*)	illness
immaginaria (*adj.*)	imaginary
penserà (*v.*, pensare *inf.*)	will think
paghi (*v.*, pagare *inf.*)	would pay
parcella (*n., f.*)	bill

Everyday English

"If my illness is imaginary, I don't think I should have to pay this bill."

Tubino

—Non sei mai contento! . . . Ieri erano troppo cotti, oggi sono troppo crudi!

Key Words

contento (*adj.*)	content
ieri (*adv.*)	yesterday
troppo (*adv.*)	too
cotti (*adj.*)	cooked
oggi (*adv.*)	today
crudi (*adj.*)	undercooked

Everyday English

[Spaghetti Out of the Box]

"You're never happy! Yesterday they were overcooked; today they're undercooked."

Matteo DeCosmo

—Hei. Ma non potevate trovare un plotone di esecuzione più efficiente . . .

Key Words

potevate (*v.*, potere *inf.*)	(you) could
trovare (*v.*, *inf.*)	find
plotone (*n.*, *m.*) di esecuzione	firing squad
più (*adv.*)	more
efficiente (*adj.*)	efficient

Everyday English

"Hey! Couldn't you find a more efficient firing squad . . ."

Enzo Scarton

OTTONE DI NOTTINGA

Ottone di Nottinga

—Ho perquisito tutto l'esercito, sire. Ed ho scoperto chi Le tirava le biglie con la fionda.
—Impiccalo.
—Ci vorrà un po' di tempo, sire. È stato tutto l'esercito.

Key Words

ho perquisito (*v.*, perquisire *inf.*)	(I) searched
esercito (*n.*, *m.*)	army
biglie (*n.*, *f.*, *pl.*)	marbles
fionda (*n.*, *f.*)	slingshot
impiccalo (*v.*, impiccare *inf.*)	hang (him)

Everyday English

Otto of Nottinga

"I've searched through the whole army, sire, and I've found out who's been using a slingshot to shoot marbles (at you)."
"Hang them."
"That will take a little time, sire. It's the entire army."

Giuliano

Eredità

—Figliolo, un giorno tutto questo bel buco nell'ozono sarà tuo.

Key Words

eredità (*n.*, *f.*)	inheritance
figliolo (*n.*, *m.* or *f.*)	child
giorno (*n.*, *m.*)	day
bel (*adj.*)	beautiful
buco (*n.*, *m.*)	hole
ozono (*n.*, *m.*)	ozone

Everyday English

Inheritance

"Child, one day this beautiful hole in the ozone will be yours."

Matteo DeCosmo

—Che strano! C'è qualcosa che non va . . . Non capisco perché
non gira . . .

Key Words

strano (*adj.*)	strange
non va (*v.*, andare *inf.*)	doesn't go, work
capisco (*v.*, capire *inf.*)	(I) understand
perché (*conj.*)	why
gira (*v.*, girare *inf.*)	roll, turn

Everyday English

"That's strange! Something is wrong . . . I don't know why it
doesn't roll . . ."

Deca

—Stava praticando una posizione yoga ed è rimasto annodato . . .

Key Words

stava praticando (*v.*, praticare *inf.*)	(he) was practicing
posizione (*n.*, *f.*)	position
rimasto (*v.*, rimanere *inf.*)	remained
annodato (*v.*, annodare *inf.*)	entangled, knotted up

Everyday English

"He was practicing a yoga position and he's stuck . . ."

Danilo

—Se vuoi proprio buttarti, fallo pure . . . ma prima togliti il vestito nuovo!

Key Words

vuoi (*v.*, volere *inf.*)	(you) want
proprio	really
buttarti (*v.*, buttarsi *inf.*) (*reflexive*)	jump off, throw yourself
fallo (*v.*, fare *inf.*)	do (it)
pure (*adv.*)	indeed
prima (*adv.*)	first
togliti (*v.*, togliere *inf.*)	remove, take off
vestito (*n., m.*)	suit
nuovo (*adj.*)	new

Everyday English

"If you really want to jump, go ahead . . . but first take off your new suit."

Matteo DeCosmo

—Fai finta di niente, Luisa . . . È capace di fare di tutto pur di farsi notare!

Key Words

fai (*v.*, fare *inf.*) finta di niente	pretend there's nothing
capace (*adj.*)	capable
fare (*v.*, *inf.*)	do
pur di	only in order to
farsi (*v.*, farsi *inf.*) notare (*v.*, *inf.*)	make himself noticed

Everyday English

"Pay no attention, Luisa. He'll do anything to be noticed!"

Ghino

—Sì, è un cane davvero ordinato!

Key Words

sì (*adv.*)	yes
cane (*n., m.*)	dog
davvero	truly
ordinato (*adj.*)	orderly, tidy

Everyday English

"Yes, he's a truly tidy dog."

Tubino

. . . Il portafoglio degli italiani continua a essere alleggerito con continui prelievi . . .

Key Words

portafoglio (*n., m.*)	wallet
continua (*v.,* continuare *inf.*)	continues
essere alleggerito (*v.,* alleggerire *inf.*)	lightened
continui (*adj.*)	continual
prelievi (*n., m., pl.*)	withdrawals

Everyday English

"The Italian wallet continues to be lightened by continual withdrawals."

Matteo DeCosmo

—Sei un essere mostruoso! Tu non prendi sul serio nemmeno il fatto che sto lasciandoti!

Key Words

circo (*n.*, *m.*)	circus
essere (*n.*, *m.*)	being
mostruoso (*adj.*)	monstrous
prendi (*v.*, prendere *inf.*) sul serio	take seriously
fatto (*n.*, *m.*)	fact
nemmeno (*adv.*)	not even
sto lasciandoti (*v.*, lasciare *inf.*)	(I) am leaving (you)

Everyday English

"You're a monster. You don't even take seriously the fact that I'm leaving you."

Matteo DeCosmo

—Sì, giullare, l'ho ricevuta la tua parcella per prestazioni professionali. Non farmi ridere!

Key Words

giullare (*n., m.*)	jester
ho ricevuta (*v.*, ricevere *inf.*)	(I) received
parcella (*n., f.*)	bill
prestazioni (*n., f., pl.*) (*sing.* prestazione)	services
professionali (*adj., pl.*)	professional
farmi (*v.*, fare *inf.*) ridere (*v., inf.*)	make (me) laugh

Everyday English

"Yes, jester, I've received your bill for professional services. Don't make me laugh."

100

Matteo DeCosmo

—Su, Enrico, non ci pensare . . . Dopo che tua moglie ti ha lasciato e dopo che sei stato licenziato, cosa pensi che ti possa capitare ancora!

Key Words

su (*adv.*)	come on, courage
dopo che (*conj.*)	after
moglie (*n., f.*)	wife
ha lasciato (*v.*, lasciare *inf.*)	left
sei stato licenziato (*v.*, licenziare *inf.*) (*passive*)	(you) were dismissed
possa (*v.*, potere *inf.*)	can, could
capitare (*v., inf.*)	happen

Everyday English

"Come on, Enrico. Don't worry about it. After your wife has left you and after you've lost your job, what else do you think could happen to you?"

Italian-English Glossary

1. Verbs are listed in their infinitive form. Reflexive verbs end in -*si*. Nouns are listed in singular form unless used in the plural (such as *calzini*, socks).
2. For additional basic words, see "Little Words" at the beginning of this book. These basic words are not listed in this glossary. You might also want to refer to the sections "Pronouns" and "Three Important Verbs," also at the beginning of this book.
3. The numbers at the right are the pages on which the words can be found.

abbaiare (v.)   bark, 39
abbigliamento (n., m.)
   clothing, 40
accettare (v.)   accept, 72
accomodarsi (v.)   have a seat, 53
acqua (n., f.)   water, 50
adesso (adv.)   now, 51
ali (n., f., pl. of ala)   wings, 53
allagamento (n., m.)
   overflowing, 33
alleggerire (v.)   lighten, 98
allora (adv.)   then, in that case, 35
alt   stop, 2
amico (n., m.)   friend, 37
amore (n., m.)   love, 5, 13
anatroccolo (n., m.)
   duckling, 38, 43, 49, 56, 62, 68, 73
anch'io   I also, me too, 13
ancora (adv.)   again, still, yet, 35, 40, 53, 58, 101
andare (v.)   go, 18, 55
animale (n., m.)   animal, 25
anno (n., m.)   year, 4, 51
annodare (v.)   entangle, knot, 94
anzi (adv.)   rather, 50
appena (adv.)   just, 47
apprezzare (v.)   appreciate, 16
arbitro (n., m.)   referee, 36

arrivare (v.)   arrive, 15, 47
articolo (n., m.)   article, 40
ascoltare (v.)   listen to, 48
assaggiare (v.)   taste, 87
assedio (n., m.)   siege, 23
assegnare (v.)   assign, 10
assicurarsi (v.)   assure oneself, 87
assolutamente (adv.)
   absolutely, 61
attimo (n., m.)   moment, 24, 31
attraversare (v.)   cross, 38
attraverso (prep.)   across, 84
aumentare (v.)   increase, 75
autostrada (n., f.)   highway, 47
avere ragione   be right, 46
avere torto   be wrong, 46
avventura (n., f.)
   adventure, 38
avvertire (v.)   warn, 52
bagnino (n., m.)   lifeguard, 54
bagno (n., m.)   bathroom, 33
banca (n., f.)   bank, 47
bastare (v.)   be enough, 74
battaglia (n., f.)   battle, 35
bau bau   bowwow (sound of dog), 39

bel (adj.)   beautiful, 92
bel tempo andato   good old times, 79
benvenuto   welcome, 81
bevanda (n., f.)   beverage, 72
Bibbia (n., f.)   Bible, 55
biglia (n., f.)   marble, 91
biscotto (n., m.)   cookie, 62
bisognare (v.)   need, 85
bisonte (n., m.)   buffalo, 41
bottiglia (n., f.)   bottle, 49, 62
bottone (n., m.)   button, 8
braccio (n., m.)   arm, 61
brevettare (v.)   patent, 53
brutto (adj.)   ugly, 38, 43, 49, 56, 62, 68, 73
bucato (adj.)   worm-eaten, 24
buco (n., m.)   hole, 92
bugiardo (n., m.)   liar, 62
buono (adj.)   good, 16
buttarsi (v.)   jump off, throw oneself, 95
cacao (n., m.)   cocoa, 62
caffè (n., m.)   coffee, 59
calcio (n., m.)   soccer, 57
calzini (n., m., pl. of calzino)   socks, 24, 55, 85
cameriere (n., m.)   waiter, 8, 59
campagna (n., f.)   countryside, 22, 79
cane (n., m.)   dog, 38, 39, 83, 97
canino (n., m.)   canine tooth, 9
capace (adj.)   capable, 96
capire (v.)   understand, 45, 61, 93
capitare (v.)   happen, 101
cara, caro (n., adj.)   dear, 12, 31, 39, 58, 63, 78, 87

carta (n., f.) di credito   credit card, 72
cartellino (n., m.)   penalty card, 36
cartello (n., m.)   sign, 20
cartolina (n., f.)   postcard, 33
casa (n., f.)   home, 43
caso (n., m.)   possibility, 21
cena (n., f.)   dinner, 2, 12
c'era una volta   once upon a time, 19, 22, 26, 38, 43, 49, 56, 62, 68, 73, 79, 83
cercare (v.)   look for, 8
certo (adv.)   undoubtedly, 5
cervello (n., m.)   brain, mind, 73
che cosa   what thing, 28
chiamare (v.)   call, 42
chiamarsi (v.)   be named, 51
chiedere (v.)   ask, ask for, 24, 36, 59
chilo (n., m.)   kilo, kilogram, 1
chiodo (n., m.)   nail, 55
cicciona (n., f.)   fat person, 77
cieco (adj.)   blind, 5
ciliegia (n., f.)   cherry, 28
ciò che (pron.)   what(ever), 36
ciotola (n., f.)   bowl, 26
cipolla (n., f.)   onion, 79
circo (n., m.)   circus, 99
cocktail (n., m.)   cocktail party, 66
coincidenza (n., f.)   coincidence, 15
collera (n., f.)   anger, 58
colone (n., m.)   colonist, 55
colonia (n., f.)   colony, 85
colpo (n., m.)   something impressive, 14
coltello (n., m.)   knife, 68
combattente (n., m.)   fighter, 7

come (*adv.*) how, as, as for, 41, 49, 56, 76

come dire how to say it, 83

come ti chiami what's your name?, 51

commercialista (*n., m.*) treasury advisor, 14

contento (*adj.*) content, 89

continuare (*v.*) continue, 98

continuo (*adj.*) continual, 98

conto (*n., m.*) bill, 48

controllo (*n., m.*) control, check, 9

convinto (*adj.*) convinced, 27

coreografo (*n., m.*) choreographer, 7

cosa pensi what do you think?, 101

costare (*v.*) cost, 17, 40

cotto (*adj.*) cooked, 89

credere (*v.*) believe, 5, 10, 51

credito (*n., m.*) credit, 72

crescere (*v.*) grow, 68

crociata (*n., f.*) Crusade, 15, 70

crociato (*n., m.*) Crusader, 70

crudo (*adj.*) undercooked, 89

cuoco (*n., m.*) cook, 49

cuore (*n., m.*) heart, 68

da che parte which way, 18

dado (*n., m.*) per brodo bouillon cube, 55

dare (*v.*) give, 64

dare (*v.*) del lei address formally, 32

da solo by oneself, 17

davanti a (*prep.*) in front of, 73

davvero (*adv.*) indeed, 83, 97

debellare (*v.*) crush, 85

delizia (*n., f.*) delight, treat, 68

dentifricio (*n., m.*) toothpaste, 55

dentista (*n., m.*) dentist, 34

dieta (*n., f.*) diet, 65

dimenticare (*v.*) forget, 34, 55

di nuovo again, 24, 67

dire (*v.*) say, tell, 3, 14, 15, 19, 22, 26, 56, 62, 75, 79, 83, 86

disperatamente (*adv.*) desperately, 60

dispiacere (*v.*) be sorry, 63

disturbarsi (*v.*) disturb oneself, 12

divertirsi (*v.*) amuse oneself, 71

divorziare (*v.*) divorce, 82

dopo che (*conj.*) after, 101

dove where, 55

dovere (*v.*) must, have to, 7, 15, 32, 55

duca (*n., m.*) duke, 61

due two, 1

dunque (*interjection*) well then, 55

durare (*v.*) last, 13

efficiente (*adj.*) efficient, 90

Elena Helen, 27

elenco (*n., m.*) list, 47

eredità (*n., f.*) inheritance, 92

ergastolo (*n., m.*) life imprisonment, 13

esecuzione (*n., f.*) execution, 2

esercito (*n., m.*) army, 91

essere (*n., m.*) being, 34, 99

fa ago, 51

fagiolo (*n., m.*) beans, 55

fame (*n., f.*) hunger, 16

famiglia (*n., f.*) family, 33, 45

fantasia (n., f.) imagination, 78

fare (v.) make, do, 6, 14, 16, 19, 26, 29, 36, 38, 45, 47, 49, 53, 61, 65, 68, 72, 74, 95, 96, 100

fare (v.) attenzione be careful, 71

fare (v.) colpo make an impression, 14

fare (v.) con comodo take one's time, 81

fare (v.) finta di niente pretend there's nothing, 96

fare (v.) visita pay a visit, 81

farsi (v.) notare make oneself noticed, 96

fatto (n., m.) fact, 99

felice (adj.) happy, 29

fenomeno (n., m.) phenomenon, 85

feroce (adj.) fierce, 85

ferocemente (adv.) fiercely, wildly, 82

festa (n., f.) party, expression of joy, 26

feudo (n., m.) fiefdom, feudal lands, 70

fidanzata (n., f.) fiancée, 5, 13, 38, 43, 49, 68, 73

fidanzato (n., m.) fiancé, 80

figlio (n., m.) child, 29

figliolo (n., m. or f.) child, 92

filo (n., m.) wire, 26

finire (v.) finish, 25

fino, fino a (prep.) until, 51, 76

fionda (n., f.) slingshot, 91

Firenze Florence, 56

fisco tax bureau (equivalent of I.R.S.), 14

fitto (n., m.) rent, 3

foglia (n., f.) leaf, 28

forchetta (n., f.) fork, 49

forse (adv.) maybe, 60

forte (adj.) strong, 59

fortuna (n., f.) luck, 41

fotografia (n., f.) photograph, 56

fresco (adj.) fresh, 72

fucile (n., m.) rifle, 55

fuggire (v.) flee, 22

fumare (v.) smoke (tobacco), 30

gamba (n., f.) leg, 61

gatto (n., m.) cat, 19, 26, 82

genitore (n., m.) parent, 64

gilè (n., m.) vest, 74

giorno (n., m.) day, 8, 92

giorno d'oggi nowadays, 39

girare (v.) roll, turn, 93

giullare (n., m.) jester, 100

giurare (v.) swear, 37

goloso (adj.) gluttonous, 62

gommone (n., m.) rubber boat, raft, 85

gonfiare (v.) inflate, 85

gradimento (n., m.) liking, 87

gradire (v.) like, 10

gran (adj.) great, 7

grazie a thanks to, 33

grosso (adj.) big, 84

guardare (v.) look, look at, 5, 35

guastarsi (v.) be broken, 4

guasto (adj.) broken, out of order, 20

guerra (n., f.) di Troia Trojan War, 27

idraulico (n., m.) plumber, 33

ieri (adv.) yesterday, 42, 89

il the (see Definite Article table)

immaginario (*adj.*)
imaginary, 88
impazzito (*adj.*)   crazy, 37
impiccare (*v.*)   hang, 91
improvvisamente (*adv.*)
suddenly, 30
incolto (*adj.*)   uncultivated,
47
incominciare (*v.*)   begin, 35
incontrare (*v.*)   meet, 67
indiano   Indian, 67
indovinare (*v.*)   guess, 78
infestato (*adj.*)   infested, 85
iniziare (*v.*)   start, 52
in modo   so that, 86
innaffiare (*v.*)   water
(something), 43
innaffiatoio (*n., m.*)
watering can, 43
in più   besides, 19
insegnare (*v.*)   teach, 25
insistere (*v.*)   insist, 53, 63
interessarsi (*v.*)   be
interested, 36
interrompere (*v.*)   interrupt,
86
intoccabile (*adj.*)
untouchable, 61
inventare (*v.*)   invent, 76
invitare (*v.*)   invite, 66
ipnotizzare (*v.*)   hypnotize,
11
isola (*n., f.*)   island, 81
kilo   kilogram (about 2.2
lbs.), 68
la   the (*see Definite Article
table*)
lacrima (*n., f.*)   tear, 79
lamentarsi (*v.*)   complain,
47
lasciare (*v.*)   let, leave, 12,
36, 70, 99, 101
leggere (*v.*)   read, 20, 25, 64
leone (*n., m.*)   lion, 84

leprotto (*n., m.*)   rabbit,
bunny, 22, 79
lettera (*n., f.*)   letter, 68
lì (*adv.*)   there, 86
licenziare (*v.*)   dismiss, 101
lince (*n., f.*)   lynx, 28
lingua (*n., f.*)   language, 39
lontano (*adj.*)   distant, 5, 13,
38, 43, 49, 68, 73
luce (*n., f.*)   light, 26
luna park (*n., m.*)
amusement park, 18
macchina (*n., f.*)
fotografica   camera, 56
madre (*n., f.*)   mother, 15, 66
magari (*adv.*)   maybe, 62
malattia (*n., f.*)   illness, 88
mandare (*v.*)   send, 33, 85
mangiare (*v.*)   eat, 21, 39
mania (*n., f.*)   mania, craze,
38, 73
mano (*n., f.*)   hand, 26, 64
mare (*n., m.*)   sea, seashore,
43, 85
marito (*n., m.*)   husband, 48
Menelao   Menelaus, 27
meno male   thank goodness,
8
mentre (*adv.*)   while, 43
meraviglioso (*adj.*)
marvelous, 36
merluzzo (*n., m.*)   codfish, 1
metro (*n., m.*)   meter (about
10 percent longer than a
yard), 41
mettere (*v.*)   put, wear, 24
**mettere (*v.*) l'anima in
pace**   get over (something),
27
mezzo (*adj.*)   half, 41
**mia/mio (*possessive
pronoun*)**   my, 82, 88
miaooo   meow (sound of cat),
39

pensare (v.)   think, 13, 36, 88, 101
pentola (n., f.)   pot, 55
perché (conj.)   why, 93
perdere (v.)   miss, lose, 57, 73
perdita (n., f.)   leak, 42
per esempio   for instance, 73
permettere (v.)   permit, 33, 61
per nulla   for anything, 57
perquisire (v.)   search, 91
pesce (n., m.) spada   swordfish, 1
peste (n., f.)   plague, 70
piangere (v.)   cry, 60
pianta (n., f.)   plant, 43
piatto (n., m.)   dish, 55
piccolo (adj.)   little, small, 38, 42, 43, 49, 56, 62, 68, 73
piccone (n., m.)   pick, 55
pigiami (n., m.)   pajamas, 55
pilota (n., m. or f.)   pilot, 52
pirata (n., m.)   pirate, 85
pistola (n., f.)   gun, 41
più (adv.)   more, 83, 90
plebeo (n., m.)   plebeian, 61
plotone (n., m.) di esecuzione   firing squad, 90
po' (poco) (pronoun)   a little, 68, 91
Polo Nord   North Pole, 38
portafoglio (n., m.)   wallet, 98
portare (v.)   take out, 44
portare (v.) via   take away, 56
posizione (n., f.)   position, 94
possibile (n.)   everything possible, 74
posticco (adj.)   artificial, 53

potere (v.)   can, be able to, could, 34, 36, 43, 61, 64, 86, 90, 101
praticare (v.)   practice, 94
pregare (v.)   beg, 69
prelievo (n., m.)   withdrawal, 98
premio Oscar   Oscar award, 41
prendere (v.)   get, 31, 41
prendere (v.) sul serio   take seriously, 99
prenotare (v.)   reserve, 9
preoccuparsi (v.)   worry, 36
preparare (v.)   prepare, 35
presentare (v.)   present, 27
prestazione (n., f.)   service, 100
prodotto (n., m.)   product, 72
professionale (adj.)   professional, 100
promettere (v.)   promise, 23
proprio (adv.)   just, exactly, really, 15, 62, 74, 95
proprio oggi   same day, 69
prossimo (adj.)   next, 40
psicologicamente (adv.)   psychologically, 35
pulci (n., f., pl. of pulce)   fleas, 19, 83
punto (n., m.)   point, 59
pur di   only in order to, 96
pure (adv.)   indeed, 95
quattro   four, 1
quattro gemelli   quadruplets, 60
quell'altro   that other, 78
quel tale che   someone who, 53
questa sera   this evening, 63
randagio (adj.)   wandering, 19
regolare (adj.)   customary, 80

repertorio (n., m.)
repertoire, 63

ricevere (v.)   receive, 100

ricordarsi (v.)   remember, 32

ridere (v.)   laugh, 6, 38, 100

ridire (v.) su   find fault with, 45

rimanere (v.)   remain, 94

rimettere (v.) a posto   put in order, 56

ringraziare (v.)   thank, 33

rinviare (v.)   postpone, 2

riparare (v.)   repair, 69

ripensare (v.)   think back, 79

riportare (v.)   take back, 2

riprendere (v.)   take up again, 30

rispondere (v.)   respond, 80

romantico (adj.)   romantic, 48

rompere (v.)   break, 61

rosmarino (n., m.)
rosemary, 22

rubinetto (n., m.)   faucet, 42

sacco (n., m.) di   lot of, 19, 26, 28, 56

sale (n., m.)   salt, 55

salmone (n., m.)   salmon, 1

saluti (n., m., pl. of saluto)
greetings, 33

salvia (n., f.)   sage, 22

sanguinario (adj.)
bloodthirsty, 85

sapere (v.)   know, 39, 40, 49, 76, 77, 84

sarà, saranno   (see "Three Important Verbs")

sarei (v., essere, conditional form)   (I) would be, 37

sartoria (n., f.)   tailor shop, 74

sbarra (n., f.)   bar, 84

scatola (n., f.)   box, 62

scendere (v.)   descend, 31

sciopero (n., m.)   strike, 52

scommettere (v.)   bet, 67

scoprire (v.)   discover, 4, 91

scrivere (v.)   write, 1, 5, 13, 38, 43, 49, 68, 73

scrupolo (n., m.)   scruple, 85

scusare (v.)   excuse, 18

sedile (n., m.)   seat, 52

se fosse a casa sua   as if you were at home, 81

sega (n., f.)   saw, 55

sembrare (v.)   seem, 11

semplice (adj.)   simple, 15

sentire (v.)   feel, hear, 39, 60, 83

serata (n., f.)   evening, 12

settimana (n., f.)   week, 40

sforzarsi (v.)   try hard, 78

siccome (adv.)   since, 17

sicuramente (adv.)   surely, 68

sicuro (adj.)   sure, 68

sigaretta (n., f.)   cigarette, 31

signor direttore (n., m.)
director, sir, 24

signorina (n., f.)   miss, 80

sino a (prep.)   even to, 59

sistema (n., m.)   system, 53

slitta (n., f.)   sled, 38

soffiare (v.)   steal, 27

sole (n., m.)   sun, 56

solitudine (n., f.)   solitude, 68

solo (adj.)   alone, 65, 83

soprattutto (adv.)   especially, above all, 16, 19, 49

spagnolo (n., m.)   Spaniard, 47

sperare (v.)   hope, expect, 81

spiacente (adj.)   sorry, 72

stamattina (adv.)   this morning, 24, 60

stare (v.)   stay, 73, 86, 91

stipendio (_n., m._) salary, 75

stoffa (_n., f._) cloth, 74

strano (_adj._) strange, 30, 93

stupendo (_adj._) stupendous, marvelous, 43

su come on, 78, 101

subacqueo (_adj._) underwater, 50

subdolo (_adj._) treacherous, deceitful, 85

subito (_adv._) soon, 31, 41

supermercato (_n., m._) supermarket, 47

tanto (_adj._) so many, 16

tappeto (_n., m._) rug, 62

tavola (_n., f._) table, 16

tedesco (_n., m._) German, 4

televisione (_n., f._) television, 76

televisore (_n., m._) television set, 4

temere (_v._) fear, 50

tempo (_n., m._) time, 56, 76, 91

terra (_n., f._) land, 47

terza volta (_n., f._) third time, 36

testa (_n., f._) head, 84

tetto (_n., m._) roof, 69

timo (_n., m._) thyme, 22

Tir (_n., m._) truck, 23

tirare (_v._) throw, 71, 91

toccare a (_v._) be one's turn, 3

togliere (_v._) remove, take off, 83, 95

tornare (_v._) return, 18, 30, 31, 66

traumatizzare (_v._) traumatize, 82

tre three, 8

tremendamente (_adv._) tremendously, 50

tronco (_n., m._) trunk (of tree), 28

troppo (_adv._) too, too much, 17, 89

trovare (_v._) find, 8, 22, 52, 69, 90

tutto da solo all by oneself, 38

urlare (_v._) howl, yell, 60

va bene all right, OK, 53

vacanze (_n., f._) vacation, 43

valigia (_n., f._) suitcase, 85

vanga (_n., f._) shovel, 55

vaso (_n., m._) vase, 26, 43, 62

vassoio (_n., m._) tray, 49

va tornare (_v._) turn back, 18

vedere (_v._) see, 26, 28, 48

vedetta (_n., f._) sentinel, scout, 28

veloce (_adj._) fast, 41

vendita (_n., f._) sale, 72

Venezia Venice, 33

venire (_v._) come, 43, 69, 70, 79, 81

veramente (_adv._) truly, 49

vero (_adj._) true, 13, 26, 56

vero? right?, 3

vestito (_n., m._) suit, 95

viaggiare (_v._) travel, 56

viaggio (_n., m._) trip, 33

viaggio (_n., m._) di nozze honeymoon, 17

visita (_n., f._) visit, appointment, 9

vita (_n., f._) lifetime, 13, 19

voglia (_n., f._) wish, desire, 22, 30

volere (_v._) want, wish, 29, 36, 38, 43, 48, 53, 65, 77, 91, 95

volo (_n., m._) flight, 53

volta (_n., f._) turn, time, 3, 5

voto (_n., m._) mark, 10

zitto (_interjection_) shut up, keep quiet, 51

English-Italian Glossary

above all   soprattutto (adv.), 16, 19, 49

absolutely   assolutamente (adv.), 61

accept   accettare (v.), 72

across   attraverso (adv.), 84

address formally   dare (v.) del lei, 32

adventure   avventura (n., f.), 38

after   dopo che (conj.), 101

again   ancora (adv.), 40, 53; di nuovo, 24, 67

ago   fa, 51

aim   mira (n., f.), 41

all by oneself   tutto da solo, 38

all right, OK   va bene, 53

alone   solo (adj.), 65, 83

amuse oneself   divertirsi (v.), 71

amusement park   luna park (n., m.), 18

anger   collera (n., f.), 58

animal   animale (n., m.), 25

appointment   visita (n., f.), 9

appreciate   apprezzare (v.), 16

arm   braccio (n., m.), 61

army   esercito (n., m.), 91

arrive   arrivare (v.), 15, 47

article   articolo (n., m.), 40

artificial   posticco (adj.), 53

as, as for   come (adv.), 41, 49

ask, ask for   chiedere (v.), 24, 36, 59

assign   assegnare (v.), 10

assure oneself   assicurarsi (v.), 87

bacon   pancetta (n., f.), 55

bank   banca (n., f.), 47

bar   sbarra (n., f.), 84

bark   abbaiare (v.), 39

bathroom   bagno (n., m.), 33

battle   battaglia (n., f.), 35

be able   potere (v.), 34, 43, 61, 64, 86, 90, 101

bean   fagiolo (n., m.), 55

beautiful   bel (adj.), 92

beg   pregare (v.), 69

begin   incominciare (v.), 35

being   essere (v.), 34

believe   credere (v.), 5, 10, 51

besides   in più, 19

best   miglior (adj.), 54

bet   scommettere (v.), 67

beverage   bevanda (n., f.), 72

Bible   Bibbia (n., f.), 55

big   grosso (adj.), 84

bill   parcella (n., f.), 88, 100; conto (n., m.), 48

black   nero (adj.), 38, 43, 49, 56, 62, 68, 73

blind   cieco (adj.), 5

bloodthirsty   sanguinario (adj.), 85

born   nascere (v.), 60

bottle   bottiglia (n., f.), 49, 62

bouillon cube   dado (n., m.) per brodo, 55

bowl   ciotola (n., f.), 26

bowwow   bau bau, 39

box   scatola (n., f.), 62

brain, mind   cervello (n., m.), 73

brat   monello (n., m.), 71

bread   pane (n., m.), 68

break   rompere (v.), 61

broken   guasto (adj.), 20

broken, be   guastarsi (v.), 4

buffalo   bisonte, 41

bunny   leprotto, 22, 79

button   bottone (n., m.), 8

by now   ormai (adv.), 27

by oneself   da solo, 17
call   chiamare (*v.*), 42
camera   macchina (*n., f.*)
fotografica, 56
can (*v.*)   potere (*v.*), 34, 36,
43, 61, 64, 86, 90, 101
canine tooth   canino (*n., m.*),
9
capable   capace (*adj.*), 96
casserole   pasticcio, 49
cat   gatto (*n., m.*), 19, 26, 82
check   controllo (*n., m.*), 9
cherry   ciliegia (*n., f.*), 28
child   figlio (*n., m.*), 29;
figliolo (*n., m.* or *f.*), 92
choreographer   coreografo
(*n., m.*), 7
cigarette   sigaretta (*n., f.*), 31
circus   circo (*n., m.*), 99
cloth   stoffa (*n., f.*), 74
clothing   abbigliamento (*n.,
m.*), 40
cocktail party   cocktail (*n.,
m.*), 66
cocoa   cacao (*n., m.*), 62
codfish   merluzzo (*n., m.*), 1
coffee   caffè (*n., m.*), 59
coincidence   coincidenza (*n.,
f.*), 15
colonist   colone (*n., m.*), 55
colony   colonia (*n., f.*), 85
come   venire (*v.*), 43, 69, 70,
79, 81
come on   su, 78, 101
complain   lamentarsi (*v.*), 47
content   contento (*adj.*), 89
continual   continuo (*adj.*),
98
continue   continuare (*v.*), 98
control   controllo (*n., m.*), 9
convinced   convinto (*adj.*),
27
cook   cuoco (*n., m.*), 49
cooked   cotto (*adj.*), 89

cookie   biscotto (*n., m.*), 62
cost   costare (*v.*), 17, 40
could   potere (*v.*), 61, 86, 90,
101
countryside   campagna (*n.,
f.*), 22, 79
craze   mania (*n., f.*), 73
crazy   impazzito (*adj.*), 37
credit   credito (*n., m.*), 72
credit card   carta (*n., f.*) di
credito, 72
cross (*v.*)   attraversare (*v.*),
38
Crusade   crociata (*n., f.*), 15,
70
Crusader   crociato (*n., m.*),
70
crush   debellare (*v.*), 85
cry   piangere (*v.*), 60
customary   regolare (*adj.*),
80
day   giorno (*n., m.*), 8, 92
dear   caro, cara (*n., adj.*), 12,
31, 39, 58, 63, 78, 87
deceitful   subdolo (*adj.*), 85
delight   delizia (*n., f.*), 68
dentist   dentista (*n., m.*), 34
descend   scendere (*v.*), 31
desire   voglia (*n., f.*), 22, 30
desperately   disperatamente
(*adv.*), 60
die   morire (*v.*), 6, 38
diet   dieta (*n., f.*), 65
dinner   cena (*n., f.*), 2, 12
director, sir   signor direttore
(*n., m.*), 24
discover   scoprire (*v.*), 4, 91
dish   piatto (*n., m.*), 55
dismiss   licenziare (*v.*), 101
distant   lontano (*adj.*), 5, 13,
38, 43, 49, 68, 73
disturb oneself   disturbarsi
(*v.*), 12
divorce   divorziare (*v.*), 82

do fare (*v.*), 19, 36, 45, 49, 65, 74, 95
doesn't go/work non va (*v.*, andare), 93
dog cane (*n., m.*), 38, 39, 83, 97
dog show mostra (*n., f.*) canina, 10
duckling anatroccolo (*n., m.*), 38, 43, 49, 56, 62, 68, 73
duke duca (*n., m.*), 61
each ogni (*adj.*), 5
eat mangiare (*v.*), 21, 39
efficient efficiente (*adj.*), 90
eight otto, 52
enough bastata (bastare, *v.*), 74
entangle annodare (*v.*), 94
especially soprattutto (*adv.*), 16, 19, 49
evening serata (*n., f.*), 12
even to sino (*prep.*), 59
every ogni (*adj.*), 5, 45
everything tutto, 49, 96
everything possible possibile (*n.*), 74
excuse scusare (*v.*), 18
execution esecuzione (*n., f.*), 2
eye occhio (*n., m.*), 28
fact fatto (*n., m.*), 99
family famiglia (*n., f.*), 33, 45
fast veloce (*adj.*), 41
fat person cicciona (*n., f.*), 77
father padre (*n., m.*), 27, 60
faucet rubinetto (*n., m.*), 42
fear temere (*v.*), 50
feel sentire (*v.*), 83
fiancé fidanzato (*n., m.*), 80
fiancée fidanzata (*n., f.*), 5, 13, 38, 43, 49, 68, 73

fiefdom, feudal lands feudo (*n., m.*), 70
fierce feroce (*adj.*), 85
fiercely ferocemente (*adv.*), 82
fighter combattente (*n., m.*), 7
find trovare (*v.*), 8, 22, 52, 90
find fault with ridire (*v.*) su, 45
finish finire (*v.*), 25
firing squad plotone (*n., m.*) di esecuzione, 90
flea pulce (*n., f.*), 19, 83
flee fuggire (*v.*), 22
flight volo (*n., m.*), 53
Florence Firenze, 56
for anything per nulla, 57
forget dimenticare (*v.*), 34, 55
for instance per esempio, 73
fork forchetta (*n., f.*), 49
four quattro, 1
fresh fresco (*adj.*), 72
friend amico (*n., m.*), 37
frying pan padella (*n., f.*), 22, 79
German tedesco (*n., m.*), 4
get prendere (*v.*), 31, 41
get over (something) mettere (*v.*) l'anima in pace, 27
give dare (*v.*), 64
gluttonous goloso (*adj.*), 62
go andare (*v.*), 18, 55
good buono (*adj.*), 16
good old times bel tempo andato, 79
great gran (*adj.*), 7
greetings saluti (*n., m., pl.*), 33
grow crescere (*v.*), 68
guess indovinare (*v.*), 78

gun pistola (n., f.), 41
half mezzo (adj.), 41
hand mano (n., f.), 26, 64
hang impiccare (v.), 91
happen capitare (v.), 101
happy felice (adj.), 29
hate odiare (v.), 82
have a seat accomodarsi (v.), 53
have to dovere (v.), 55
head testa (n., f.), 84
hear sentire (v.), 39, 60
heart cuore (n., m.), 68
Helen Elena, 27
highway autostrada (n., f.), 47
hole buco (n., m.), 92
home casa (n., f.), 43
honeymoon viaggio (n., m.) di nozze, 17
horrible orribile (adj.), 61
hour ora (n., f.), 44
how come (adv.), 56, 76
howl urlare (v.), 60
how to say come dire, 83
hunger fame (n., f.), 16
husband marito (n., m.), 48
hypnotize ipnotizzare (v.), 11
I also anch'io, 13
illness malattia (n., f.), 88
imaginary immaginario (adj.), 88
imagination fantasia (n., f.), 78
increase aumentare (v.), 75
indeed pure (adv.), 95; davvero (adv.), 83, 97
Indian indiano, 67
infested infestato (adj.), 85
inflate gonfiare (v.), 85
in front of davanti a (prep.), 73

inheritance eredità (n., f.), 92
insist insistere (v.), 53, 63
interested, be interessarsi (v.), 36
interrupt interrompere (v.), 86
in that case allora (adv.), 35
invent inventare (v.), 76
invite invitare (v.), 66
island isola, 81
jester giullare (n., m.), 100
jump off buttarsi (v.), 95
just appena (adv.), 47; proprio (adv.), 15
keep quiet zitto (interjection), 51
kilo, kilogram chilo/kilo (n., m.), 1, 68
knife coltello (n., m.), 68
know sapere (v.), 39, 40, 49, 76, 77, 84
land terra (n., f.), 47
language lingua (n., f.), 39
last durare (v.), 13
laugh ridere (v.), 6, 38, 100
leaf (n.) foglia (n., f.), 28
leak perdita (n., f.), 42
leave lasciare (v.), 12, 70, 99, 101; partire (v.), 15, 17
leg gamba (n., f.), 61
let lasciare (v.), 12, 36, 70, 99, 101
let (someone) come in fare (v.) entrare (v.), 53
letter lettera (n., f.), 68
liar bugiardo (n., m.), 62
lifeguard bagnino (n., m.), 54
life imprisonment ergastolo (n., m.), 13
lifetime vita (n., f.), 13, 19

only in order to   pur di, 96

opportunistic   opportunisto (*adj.*), 26

orderly   ordinato (*adj.*), 97

Oscar Award   premio Oscar, 41

out of order   guasto (*adj.*), 20

overflowing   allagamento (*n., m.*), 33

oyster   ostrica (*n., f.*), 1

ozone   ozono (*n., m.*), 92

pajamas   pigiami (*n., m.*), 55

parachute   paracadute (*n., m.*), 52

parent   genitore (*n., m.*), 64

parking lot   parcheggio (*n., m.*), 47

pass   passare (*v.*), 43, 76, 84

patent (*v.*)   brevettare (*v.*), 53

pay   pagare (*v.*), 12, 88

pay a visit   fare (*v.*) visita, 81

pay for oneself   pagarsi (*v.*), 33

pay no attention   fare (*v.*) finta di niente, 96

penalty card   cartellino (*n., m.*), 36

permit   permettere (*v.*), 33, 61

phenomenon   fenomeno (*n., m.*), 85

photograph   fotografia (*n., f.*), 56

pick (*n.*)   piccone (*n., m.*), 55

pilot   pilota (*n., m.* or *f.*), 52

pirate   pirata (*n., m.*), 85

plague   peste (*n., f.*), 70

plant   pianta (*n., f.*), 43

plebeian   plebeo (*n., m.*), 61

plumber   idraulico (*n., m.*), 33

point   punto (*n., m.*), 59

position   posizione (*n., f.*), 94

possibility   caso (*n., m.*), 21

postcard   cartolina (*n., f.*), 33

postpone   rinviare (*v.*), 2

pot   pentola (*n., f.*), 55

practice   praticare (*v.*), 94

prepare   preparare (*v.*), 35

present   presentare (*v.*), 27

product   prodotto (*n., m.*), 72

professional   professionale (*adj.*), 100

promise   promettere (*v.*), 23

psychologically   psicologicamente (*adv.*), 35

put in order   rimettere (*v.*) a posto, 56

quadruplets   quattro gemelli (*n., m., pl.*), 60

rabbit   leprotto (*n., m.*), 22, 79

raft   gommone (*n., m.*), 85

rather   anzi (*adv.*), 50

read   leggere (*v.*), 20, 25, 64

really   proprio, 62, 74, 95

receive   ricevere (*v.*), 100

referee   arbitro (*n., m.*), 36

remain   rimanere (*v.*), 94

remember   ricordarsi (*v.*), 32

remove   togliere (*v.*), 95

rent   fitto (*n., m.*), 3

repair   riparare (*v.*), 69

repertoire   repertorio (*n., m.*), 63

reserve   prenotare (*v.*), 9

respond   rispondere (*v.*), 80

return   tornare (*v.*), 18, 30, 31, 66

rifle   fucile (*n., m.*), 55

right?   vero?, 3

right, to be   avere (*v.*) ragione, 46

roll   girare (*v.*), 93

romantic romantico (*adj.*), 48
roof tetto (*n., m.*), 69
rosemary rosmarino (*n., m.*), 22
rubber boat gommone (*n., m.*), 85
rug tappeto (*n., m.*), 62
safe sicuro (*adj.*), 68
safely, surely sicuramente (*adv.*), 68
sage salvia (*n., f.*), 22
salary stipendio (*n., m.*), 75
sale vendita (*n., f.*), 72
salmon salmone (*n., m.*), 1
salt sale (*n., m.*), 55
same day proprio oggi, 69
saw sega (*n., f.*), 55
say dire (*v.*), 3, 14, 15, 19, 22, 26, 56, 62, 75, 79, 83, 86
scruple scrupolo (*n., m.*), 85
sea, seashore mare (*n., m.*), 43, 85
search perquisire (*v.*), 91
seat sedile (*n., m.*), 52
see vedere (*v.*), 26, 28, 48
seem sembrare (*v.*), 11
send mandare (*v.*), 33, 85
sentinel vedetta, 28
service prestazione (*n., f.*), 100
shadow ombra (*n., f.*), 73
shovel vanga (*n., f.*), 55
shut up zitto (*interjection*), 51
siege assedio (*n., m.*), 23
sign cartello (*n., m.*), 20
silent muto (*adj.*), 86
simple semplice (*adj.*), 15
since siccome (*adv.*), 17
sled slitta (*n., f.*), 38
slingshot fionda (*n., f.*), 91
small piccolo (*adj.*), 38, 42, 43, 49, 56, 62, 68, 73

smoke (tobacco) fumare (*v.*), 30
snowball palla (*n., f.*) di neve, 71
soccer calcio (*n., m.*), 57
socks calzini (*n., m., pl.*), 24, 55
solitude solitudine (*n., f.*), 68
someone who quel tale che, 53
soon subito, 31, 41
sorry spiacente (*adj.*), 72
sorry, be dispiacere (*v.*), 63
so that in modo, 86
Spaniard spagnolo (*n., m.*), 47
speak parlare (*v.*), 4, 12, 25, 29, 37, 47, 64
start iniziare (*v.*), 52
stay stare (*v.*), 73, 86
steal soffiare (*v.*), 27
still ancora (*adv.*), 40, 58, 101
stop alt, 2
strange strano (*adj.*), 30, 93
strike sciopero (*n., m.*), 52
strong forte (*adj.*), 59
stupendous stupendo (*adj.*), 43
suddenly improvvisamente (*adv.*), 30
suit vestito (*n., m.*), 95
suitcase valigia (*n., f.*), 85
sun sole (*n., m.*), 56
supermarket supermercato (*n., m.*), 47
swear giurare (*v.*), 37
swordfish pesce (*n., m.*) spada, 1
system sistema (*n., m.*), 53
table tavola (*n., f.*), 16
tailor shop sartoria (*n., f.*), 74

untouchable   intoccabile
(*adj.*), 61
urchin   monello (*n., m.*), 71
vacation   vacanze (*n., f.*), 43
vase   vaso (*n., m.*), 26, 43, 62
vegetable soup   minestra (*n.,
f.*), 8
Venice   Venezia, 33
very much   moltissimo
(*adv.*), 36
vest   gilè (*n., m.*), 74
visit (n.)   visita (*n., f.*), 9
visit (v.)   trovare (*v.*), 69
waiter   cameriere (*n., m.*), 8,
59
walk   passeggio (*n., m.*), 44
wallet   portafoglio (*n., m.*), 98
wandering   randagio (*adj.*), 19
want   volere (*v.*), 29, 36, 38,
43, 48, 53, 65, 77, 91, 95
warn   avvertire (*v.*), 52
water   acqua (*n., f.*), 50
water (something)
innaffiare (*v.*), 43
watering can   innaffiatoio
(*n., m.*), 43
wear   mettere (*v.*), 24
week   settimana (*n., f.*), 40
welcome   benvenuto, 81
well then   dunque
(*interjection*), 55

what do you think   cosa
pensi, 101
what(ever)   ciò che, 36
what thing   che cosa, 28
what's your name?   come ti
chiami, 51
where   dove, 55
which way   da che parte, 18
while   mentre (*adv.*), 43
why   perché (*conj.*), 93
wife   moglie (*n., f.*), 4, 24, 82,
101
wildly   ferocemente (*adj.*), 82
wings   ali (*n., f., pl.*), 53
wire   filo (*n., m.*), 26
wish (v.)   volere (*v.*), 29, 38,
43, 53, 65, 77, 91, 95
wish (n.)   voglia (*n., f.*), 22, 30
withdrawal   prelievo (*n., m.*),
98
world   mondo (*n., m.*), 56, 57
worm-eaten   bucato (*adj.*), 24
worry   preoccuparsi (*v.*), 36
write   scrivere (*v.*), 1, 5, 13,
38, 43, 49, 68, 73
wrong, to be   avere (*v.*) torto,
46
year   anno (*n., m.*), 51
yell   urlare (*v.*), 60
yesterday   ieri (*adv.*), 42, 89
yet   ancora (*adv.*), 35, 101

FOREIGN LANGUAGE BOOKS

Multilingual
The Insult Dictionary: How to Give 'Em Hell in 5 Nasty Languages
The Lover's Dictionary: How to be Amorous in 5 Delectable Languages
Handbook for Multilingual Business Writing
Multilingual Phrase Book
Let's Drive Europe Phrasebook
Talk Your Way Around Europe Phrasebook
Thomas Cook European Rail Traveler's Phrasebook
CD-ROM "Languages of the World": Multilingual Dictionary Database

Spanish
NTC's Beginner's Spanish and English Dictionary
Vox Spanish and English Dictionaries
Cervantes-Walls Spanish and English Dictionary
NTC's Dictionary of Spanish False Cognates
Nice 'n Easy Spanish Grammar
Spanish Verbs and Essentials of Grammar
Spanish Grammar in Review
Getting Started in Spanish
Spanish Culture Coloring Book
El Alfabeto
Spanish à la Cartoon
101 Spanish Idioms
Guide to Spanish Idioms
Guide to Spanish Suffixes
Guide to Correspondence in Spanish
The Hispanic Way
Al Corriente: Expressions Needed for Communicating in Everyday Spanish

French
NTC's New College French and English Dictionary
French Verbs and Essentials of Grammar
Real French
Getting Started in French
Guide to French Idioms
Guide to Correspondence in French
French Culture Coloring Book
L'Alphabet
French à la Cartoon
101 French Idioms
Nice 'n Easy French Grammar
NTC's Beginner's French and English Dictionary
NTC's Dictionary of Faux Amis
NTC's Dictionary of Canadian French
NTC's French and English Business Dictionary
Au courant: Expressions for Communicating in Everyday French
The French Way

German
Schöffler-Weis German and English Dictionary
NTC's Beginner's German and English Dictionary
Klett German and English Dictionary
Klett Super-Mini German and English Dictionary
Guide to Correspondence in German
Getting Started in German
German Verbs and Essentials of Grammar
Guide to German Idioms
Streetwise German
Nice 'n Easy German Grammar
German à la Cartoon
NTC's Dictionary of German False Cognates

Italian
Zanichelli Super-Mini Italian and English Dictionary
Zanichelli New College Italian and English Dictionary
NTC's Beginner's Italian and English Dictionary
Getting Started in Italian
Italian Verbs and Essentials of Grammar
The Italian Way

Greek
NTC's New College Greek and English Dictionary

Latin
Essentials of Latin Grammar
Teach Yourself Latin

Hebrew
Everyday Hebrew

Chinese
Easy Chinese Phrasebook and Dictionary
Basic Chinese Vocabulary Dictionary

Korean
Korean in Plain English

Polish
The Wiedza Powszechna Compact Polish and English Dictionary

Swedish
Swedish Verbs and Essentials of Grammar

Russian
Easy Russian Phrasebook and Dictionary
Complete Handbook of Russian Verbs
NTC's Compact Russian and English Dictionary
Essentials of Russian Grammar
Business Russian
Roots of the Russian Language
Basic Structure Practice in Russian
The Russian Way

Japanese
Easy Japanese
Easy Kana Workbook
Easy Hiragana
Easy Katakana
101 Japanese Idioms
Konnichi wa Japan
NTC's Dictionary of Japan's Cultural Code Ways
Japanese in Plain English
Everyday Japanese
Japanese for Children
Japanese Cultural Encounters
Japanese for the Travel Industry
Nissan's Business Japanese

"Just Enough" Phrase Books
Chinese, Dutch, French, German, Greek, Hebrew, Hungarian, Italian, Japanese,
   Portuguese, Russian, Scandinavian, Serbo-Croat, Spanish
Business French, Business German, Business Spanish
BBC Phrase Books
   French, Spanish, German, Italian, Greek, Arabic, Turkish, Portuguese

Audio and Video Language Programs
Just Listen 'n Learn Spanish, French, German, Italian, Japanese, Greek, and Arab
   Business Spanish, Business French, Business German, Arabi, Turkish
Just Listen 'n Learn...Spanish, French, German PLUS
Speak...Spanish, French, German, Japanese, Russian
Conversational...Spanish, French, German, Italian, Russian, Greek, Japanese, Tha
   Portuguese in 7 Days
Practice & Improve Your...Spanish, French, Italian, and German
Practice & Improve Your...Spanish, French, Italian, and German PLUS
Improve Your...Spanish, French, Italian, and German: The P&I Method
VideoPassport French
VideoPassport Spanish
How to Pronounce...Spanish, French, German, Italian, Russian, Japanese Correct
Verb Drill Series
   French, Spanish, German, Italian
By Association Series
   Spanish, French, German, Italian
How to Pronounce Series
   Spanish, French

PASSPORT BOOKS
a division of *NTC Publishing Group*
Lincolnwood, Illinois USA